SO WHO DO YOU THINK YOU ARE?

Discover Your Authentic Value

Mpumi Mabuza

So Who Do You Think You Are?
Copyright © Mpumi Mabuza 2019
The moral right of the author has been asserted.

Prepared for print by Preflight Books, Pretoria,
a division of BK Publishing (Pty) Ltd
www.bkpublishing.co.za

Cover design: Alex-Paige Green
Book design: Micaela de Freitas

Author Photograph: Ronnie Hall, iDesign Photography
Author dressed by Khomotso Nkambule, What's The Occassion

ISBN -13
978-0-620-82978-6

CONTENTS

DEDICATION

This book is dedicated to the life and legacy of Drs Myles and Ruth Ann Munroe. Papa, you told me there is greatness on the inside of me - and I believed you. You are a true leader because you saw potential in me that I could not see. It's like you reached in, pulled out my authentic self and reintroduced me to myself. You were constantly demanding, pulling and expecting more out of me – daring me to think beyond my perceived limitations. Thank you for being the people you were and for allowing yourselves to be used by the Creator the way He did. I know I speak not only for myself but also for many when I say indeed your lives bear testimony to how much He loves us.

To the Creator's most precious creation – the human being; for whom my desire and passion is that they realise and celebrate their authentic value.

To the Source and Sustainer of my authentic and purposeful value, the Omnipotent and Omniscient One, I thank You for the privilege of being Your vessel.

ACKNOWLEDGEMENTS

This work is a culmination of various inputs from people who have taught me, both directly and indirectly. I am grateful for your mentorship, books, phone calls, messages, and assuring words of encouragement. Thank you for caring enough to hold me accountable. Your commitment to continuously recognise the potential in me and help me realise my own value has inspired me to do the same for others. You will forever be an invaluable part of my life.

My heartfelt and deepest gratitude to my husband Eric, and our children, Lulama and Lithemba, for their steadfast love, support, understanding, and patience during the countless hours I spent to bring this vision to life. Thank you for believing in me, and for selflessly allowing me the freedom to pursue my purpose. You truly are an inspiration and my number one fans.

FOREWORD

Through this book, the author addresses two fundamental, all time and universal questions about being and living of humankind. Any kind of answer to these two questions results in a lifestyle which affects not only the quality of health but also the development and peace of individuals and their families and communities. There are many ways of answering these questions which include their denial, unconscious, reactive and unintentional mode of facing these challenges. The author supports that a conscious and intentional meaning orientated way of responding to these questions promote health and prevent ill health.

Our current context or environment of increased social isolation despite the latest development in communication and transport, prevailing interpersonal disconnection due to our high mobility, conflicts and wars and rise of life threatening and chronic diseases despite the advance of our medical technology creates and entertains a sense of psychosocial dizziness or confusion. The violence and the displacement of people observed all over the world continues to disrupt many communities and their traditions. The social isolation, interpersonal disconnection and poor health with its suffering and losses added to the fragmentation of communities and their cultures result in many people experiencing what one might call psycho-socio-cultural disorientation. This experience of psycho-socio-cultural disorientation renders the dealing with the questions of being and living a very challenging task.

In addressing these two universal questions of humankind, this book is relevant and appealing to all. It is relevant to the witnesses and bystanders of suffering, and the sufferers themselves. It confronts the perpetrators of all forms of violence and their victims. It speaks to the "have's" and "have not's". It engages the academics, the philosophers and the ordinary person in the street equally.

The author succeeds to accomplish a major endeavour of engaging both the religious and the non-religious through her writing despite her firm conviction in a creator of humankind. With this belief, the author has managed to transcend the religious barriers and focus on the questions simply as a human being who connects to all.

In a unique and authentic way, the author writes with courage and clarity. The author shares her personal experiences and life lessons with care of her readers. Through the book, the author proposes first what we are not and then suggests ways of being who we are made to be. This book is an appeal to each of us to live life as authentic beings with meaning and purpose.

Dr Kanda MA

Medical Doctor in Community Mental Health, West Rand Health District, Gauteng, South Africa

Logotherapy Facilitator, Centre for Applied Psychology, UNISA

Board Member of the Viktor Frankl Institute, South Africa

E-Tutor Department of Anthropology, UNISA

ENDORSEMENTS

First of all thank you for honouring and dedicating this book to my Dad Dr Myles Munroe and Mother, Mama Ruth Munroe, whom I had the privilege of working with and was mentored by for over 25 years.

It is fascinating to see how Mpumi is used by God to challenge humanity in their quest for self-discovery and the best life God prepared for each one of us. In this book we are encouraged to discover our full potential and to see ourselves the way God sees us. He created us in His image and likeness. We also learn that the dominion mandate is not for a selected few but was given to all humans in the planet, including those who are intimidated to become them self.

So Who Do You Think You Are gives a unique, both kingdom and motivational perspective on the challenges of discovery of self and unlocking human value faced by human beings today. She enlightens us to the value God placed in humans; the apex of His creation. We are also reminded that God put His precious image and likeness in man, which makes the human being the most precious creation of all. Anyone who reads this book will not remain the same, I guarantee you. When you read these pages, they will expand your thinking and the way you look at God's creation called Mankind.

Mpumi learned well from Dr Myles Munroe to become the author she is today and I would recommend anything written by her.

Mr Charlie Masala
CEO
Myles Munroe International-Africa

Mpumi has once again showed us her tremendous insight and dynamic inspiration in this work focusing in on understanding your true identity. Unfortunately many people live and die and never discover who they really are and what they were born to do, and thus they live unfulfilled almost meaningless lives. Their tombstones are likely to read, "I was here". For those who discover their true identity they in turn will die empty, because the world would have benefited from their discovery of their gift and purpose. Mpumi shows us the journey of discovery, the dynamics of development and the fulfilment of dominating in destiny.

Dr Dave Burrows
Senior Pastor, Bahamas Faith Ministries International, Bahamas

---

To those who want to live beyond their limitations, this book is replete with great principles and truths that will unlock potential and propel you towards your God-given purpose. Formatted as a training manual, it is loaded with great practical principles and truths that anyone can apply in everyday life.

Pastor Maureen B Shana
Founder: Woman Unlimited & Unlocking Potential Consulting
Co- Founder Word of Life International Ministries

Yet another daring book! Mpumi's authentic stance on unleashing human potential is so plainly articulated in this book. The greatest gift that Mpumi has, is that of expressing her thoughts with ease and yet so full of cogency that causes the reader to be absorbed and find resonance in the subject at hand. Her undisputed narrating ability has given this book a flavour like no other; she has so beautifully imbued and interweaved events and stories to enrich her book principal thought.

I could not agree with her more, that, to simply just exist being dictated to by reduced views or opinions, is rather an act of thievery. When we allow this our functionality gets negatively interfered with, which is a serious societal indictment. It thwarts our creative value to the world, and this value is indeed crucial as in the words of Dr Viktor Frankl, it is one of the ways in which humans could find meaning in life. It is not a secret that countless people, who although, still breathing, have unfortunately unconsciously resigned from maximizing themselves. Many have fallen prey to this reductionism of our age where limited views of ourselves or others have caused enormous damage, deprivation and immobilisation.

Mpumi through her book, *So Who Do You Think You Are* has made a clarion call for us to heed the constant and true voice, that beckon us to realize the freedom of choice that is forever present in every moment of our life journey. The choice is to say 'Yes' to who we truly are on the inside.

One take away from this book is that no single person can ever succeed beyond the level of his or her knowledge. This book is provoking us to daringly question a range of 'accepted normal issues', such as our view of self and the world and faulty knowledge bases that have for the longest time messed up our identity descriptor. Reality is, even if God has best intentions about us and who we ought to be, that could be nullified as long as the channel through which we receive from Him is marred.

Reverend Musa Lalamani

Executive Director, Mudinda Consultancy Group

Logotherapy Research Supervisor

Life Coach and Author

The beauty of humanity is in its complexity. Even when we are in an active relationship with our Creator, many of us embark on our life journey with tools that need fixing or replacement. This can be in the form of relationships or environments, and most importantly our sense of self, and the identities we embody. Along the way we need to learn how to appreciate our cracks, bulges and loose screws. With that in mind, this book is phenomenal because it has been written to mean different things to different people. Through utilising a biopsychosocial spiritual approach, the author has captivated the essence of humanity in a unique and practical way. Exploring the words in this book, let them resonate with your life experience and meet you where you are. The author's personal accounts reflect just how dynamic and tumultuous the life trajectory really is. As you read it, let it speak to you, let the words dig into your soul and make you smile, make you weep, make you angry, make you celebrate. Be intrigued by your authenticity! The greatest power of this book is that it reminds you that you have been created with resilience and agency to walk your life journey, your way… and your authenticity is the one thing you will always be a success at.

This book compels you to ask yourself the questions that you may not have known actually existed. You have been created to be a superpower, and your communities are waiting for you…

This book fed my soul and spoke to me as a human being and as a therapist, especially right now.

Amina Mwaikambo
Intern Psychologist
Centre for the Study of Violence and Reconciliation Trauma Clinic

PROLOGUE

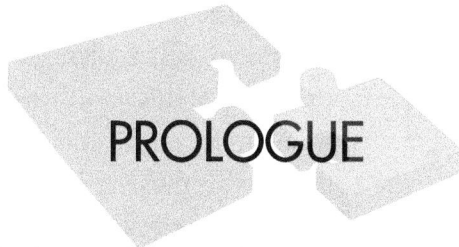

The Original Intent

That which is created can only know and understand itself
fully through its creator, without whom it would not exist in
the first place; for its original existence was in its creator's
mind even before it manifested in the physical

All things have the same components and essence as their
source. Synonyms for the word source include origin, root,
author, initiator, architect and manufacturer. The Greek word for
source is Arche, which translates to 'beginning', 'origin' or 'first
cause'. So the source of an item must have existed before it, so that
it may produce the item and bring it to existence.

It is therefore safe to say that a product cannot be greater than its
source, for it is through its source that it came to exist.

So the created thing now exists – but it does not end there; in
fact, that is only the beginning. Everything that was created was
created for a purpose. God, our Creator, created you and me

with a purpose in mind; and that purpose, is the reason why we are alive. Not only did He assign purpose to us – He went on to endow us with all we will need to accomplish that purpose. He packed us with all manner of gifts and talents, even right down to our physical appearance to ensure this. In other words, He built us for success in our assignment; therefore, it is our responsibility to operate within the boundaries of those assignments, otherwise, we will malfunction. Now, I thought I might add, that it is impossible to separate yourself from your purpose. Trying to do so would be a waste of time, energy and even resources in some cases. Can a clay pot dictate to its potter how it should be fashioned and why? No! You and your purpose are one – there is (or should be) no distinction. Your success lies in fulfilling only the purpose assigned to you by your Creator, not the 'self-assigned purpose'. I have never heard of a manufacturer of a product who intentionally sets it up for failure and I remain curious to hear if anyone has. No creator would do this – and why you may ask? It is because their **name** and **reputation** depend on the performance and ultimate success of their product. That is why they make sure that their product comes fully loaded with all the potential it will need to succeed. We all have the potential to fulfil our purpose. Simply put, this means that you and I are wired for success because our Creator's name and reputation depend on it. How amazing is that?

A short while after coming to this realisation, I coined this quote: "As flight is to the bird and as swim is to the fish, so is your purpose to you". Think about it, you can 'fire' a bird from a lot of things but never from flying. It will always fly no matter what because it was 'built to fly'. You would have to forcefully hurt or restrict it somehow to hinder it from flying. The same goes for the swimming fish, as long as it is in water. Sometimes purpose-in-action can be quite the 'thorn in the side' or an irritant for others until they get to appreciate its diversity.

Have you ever woken up in the middle of the night from a deep and glorious sleep by a dog's incessant barking? If you are a light sleeper like me, out of sheer frustration, you probably start imagining ways to silence it, knowing very well you couldn't go through with it. Then, I began to think about why the dog was barking so tirelessly and sometimes, it would seem, at nothing, and came to the realization that barking is what a dog does; it was 'built for barking'. So, I could either just deal with it or try to avoid situations where I could be woken up by barking dogs. Another example is birds. The one thing that birds are gifted at doing is to sing, especially pretty early in the morning. They have this special ability to perch on your bedroom windowsill and joyfully proceed to hit extremely high notes, the kind of pitch that you never thought possible; usually during the last hour or two before it is time to wake up... I will say no more! Again, this is what birds do! It would probably be better and less stressful to just enjoy the melody than trying to fight it. At least that is what I concluded.

Our gifts come with certain boundaries or terms and conditions, that each of us must operate within in order to succeed in our assignments. Imagine for a moment, a fish trying to swim outside of water or a bird attempting to fly underwater – both would not survive, they would die. This same principle also applies to every created thing. Normally, every product comes with a user's manual, which then tells you how to and how not to operate the product. Why is the manual important, you may ask? Well, because it contains the mind, heart and thoughts of the Inventor concerning his product. For example, when the manual says, 'do not operate in or close to water' then you know that if you attempt to do that, the product will malfunction because no one knows it better than its creator. So you and I need to endeavour to live lives that are conducive to fulfilling our purpose. We have that responsibility.

Having said that, I feel it is imperative for us to understand that although we were created for a purpose, that purpose is made up of many different moments or seasons. This means that while your purpose will not change, 'how' you attain it, however, may vary. We often make the mistake of thinking that purpose can only be realised in only one significant moment and judge ourselves (and others) harshly when we feel this was either not achieved or under-achieved. We fall into the trap of compartmentalising our entire existence into just one moment. The truth is, life is made up of many different, yet significant moments (both the good and the bad); and every moment counts and must be explored to the fullest extent. Let's look at the following example to illustrate this adequately: take a lightbulb, which is tasked to illuminate a room. This lightbulb shines a light that is made up of various colours and gives vibrant colour to the room, which it achieves in phases. The different colours, which seem to appear at the same time, each give a unique ambience to the room. The lightbulb is 'secretly' connected to many different wires, which in essence 'carry' the power to it; but does this in stages to give off the unique colour at a unique time. So, the **purpose** here is to illuminate the room but in order for that purpose to be realised, all those wires are necessary to play their different roles in bringing the different coloured lights at the right moment. So for whatever reason, in this example you can change or interchange the wires to add more, to reduce, to improve or even to replace the colours; but the purpose of the bulb does not change – it is still to illuminate the room. Another important observation is that while the wires may vary in their function, they are all equally important because, without one, the collective effect would not be the same. They make the different moments of this purpose equally significant! We do not (and should not) live only for and in the moment when the lightbulb illuminates the room but also live in the varying moments that make it possible for the lightbulb to illuminate the room.

Hence, we need to do whatever it takes to create a healthy environment for us to achieve our purpose, be it eating right, exercising, acquiring more knowledge, attending seminars, etc. Whilst it is true that we were all created to succeed in our different assignments, it is equally true that that success can only be realised if we operate under the conditions stipulated by our Architect, who knows us better than anyone ever could. So if you are a fish, for example, do not attempt to leave the water. Whenever you feel you want to understand yourself better, it will prove more beneficial and efficient to look to your Inventor, rather than the invention. There are so many instances in which we try to find answers concerning our lives from other people, who (by the way) are also created just like we are. We seek validation and acceptance from these people and allow their words and opinions to be the final authority in our lives. These could be, for example, parents, teachers, mentors, spouses, siblings, friends, enemies, employers, therapists and other professionals. Just to clarify, I am not saying that the opinions of other people do not matter or are not important; I am saying that they are not and should not be the standard and final authority over your life. Why? As they did not invent you, they do not know you or how you should operate. Although it is good and even advisable to seek advice and guidance from other people when needed, you should always check with your Inventor. What He has said concerning you is the ultimate standard. Remember that **you are not your opinion of yourself and neither are you other people's opinion of yourself.**

The key to understanding life is in the source of life and not in the life itself. You will never know yourself by relating to the creation but only to the Creator. Not relating to the Creator not only causes us to be ignorant of our identity but also our position in terms of our purpose and our confidence to fulfil said purpose.

This book is about addressing the question of who we really are as humans but in order to adequately answer that question, perhaps we need to first address who we are not!

WHO YOU ARE NOT

CHAPTER 1

You Are Not Your Past, Present, Or Future

FREEDOM IS WHAT YOU DO WITH WHAT HAS BEEN DONE TO YOU

~JEAN PAUL SARTRE

L abels often come from different and for the most part, unfortunate situations which include colonialism, slavery, background, past experiences, etc. and they can either be societal or even self-imposed. Each and every one of us has at least one story to tell that is unique to us. I remember being ten years of age in the fifth grade. On this particular day, our class teacher was absent and one of the senior students, a prefect, was assigned to our class. As he began to give us math problems to solve from our workbooks, I realised that there was something I did not fully understand and needed more clarity on, so I shot my hand up to ask a question. Instead of answering my question, he made a comment about my voice which did not sound like a compliment to a ten-year-old child. Chuckling, he said that my voice did not sound like a girl's voice. He said it was deep and sounded like that of a boy. Whether or not there was intentional malice behind the comment or just a bad 'joke' from his side, I will never know. What I do know, however, is what happened next. He had the rest of the class laughing, pointing towards my direction and making unkind comments.

Hurt and embarrassed, I cried for the rest of the day and when my Dad came to pick us up from school, I tearfully relayed the story to him. He emphatically told me, "What you heard is both unfortunate and untrue and I am sorry that you had to hear it. I am your dad and I would know if your voice was deep and boyish and it is not! So do not believe the lie. I will call your class teacher and take it up with her". I must admit, I did feel better after that. My dad always had a way to do just that. He felt strongly that a parent would know (or should know) their child better than anyone else. Up to this day, I have never followed up on whether that phone call was made or not. My dad had said it was not true and promised to handle the situation, so all was well again – or so I thought. To most people, this may not sound like something to be hung up on, but not even the comfort that came after the 'pep talk' from my well-intentioned father could protect me from what would happen for the next ten to fifteen years. I only realised this long after I graduated and started working. To this day, I am not sure exactly what brought it up but one day I was reminded that for the most part, I never really asked questions in class from that day in primary school, right up until my junior years in university. Mind you, this was not because I did not have anything to say or ask. I remember many times when I had a question in my mind and at the tip of my tongue but just could not muster the courage to shoot my hand up and ask. Even in group settings, I would always try to make sure I was not appointed as the spokesperson for the group so that I did not have to speak publicly. Needless to say, I did a lot of blending in with the crowd for years. I was so afraid of something that had happened well over a decade before. Sadly, though specific details may vary, my story is not all too unfamiliar to most of us.

Too many times I have met people from different walks of life, young and old, who attribute their current situations and/or their past to consequences of unfavourable events that happened before. For some of them, it has been (and still is) a journey that has seen them go through much-needed counselling and even physical therapy. One cannot even begin to imagine the atrocities that people are subjected to every day. Having said that, I must also say that every situation we face provides us with a unique opportunity to choose how we will respond to it. The following anonymous quote bears witness, "We are continually faced by great opportunities brilliantly disguised as insoluble problems."

Keeping in mind that suffering is an unavoidable part of life; we must decide to respond to life's questions the right way. In his book, *Man's Search for Meaning*, Viktor Frankl says this during the dark days of his imprisonment in the German concentration camps, "We had to learn ourselves, and furthermore, we had to teach the despairing man the it did not really matter what we expected from life but rather what life expected from us". He goes on to say, "Life ultimately means taking the responsibility to find the right answer to its problems and to fulfil the tasks which it constantly sets for each individual". As living, breathing human beings, you and I are constantly faced with all aspects of life: the good and the bad but more specifically the bad. The good news is that we have also been gifted with the ability to decide our reality in any situation, which is that **there is more to us than what other people have said and done.** That is how we are to respond in these situations, and we are able to do so.

You are not what society has labelled or classified you to be. Most of the time we get so caught up in the labels that we forget our function, which comes from our purpose. The one thing about labels is that they are not fixed; they are transitory and therefore useless to hang on to. Your teacher or parent may call you stupid and tell you that you will never amount to anything – and what is your response to that? The correct response should be to continue to acquire knowledge and study to improve yourself, not for them but for all who will benefit from your gift. I say correct response because there could be other responses like being despondent and discouraged to the point of giving up. I once heard a story from someone I love and respect (whom I will refer to as P) of how, as a young boy in the 1960s, he was berated by his teacher, telling him that he was failing his subject and would continue to fail. The reason he gave was that his student's brain was small like a monkey's and so he could not process thoughts and solve problems like other humans; therefore, he must save his parent's money and forget about school, because he is wasting both their time – he will never amount to anything significant. Well, the young boy grew up and became a man; he grew not only in stature but in wisdom too and became known all over the world. You see, he did not let his teacher's opinion of him dictate his future. He did not allow that situation to negate, stunt, stifle or even determine the depth of his potential. For a while he was crushed, yes, he came very close to believing those words and making them his reality. In the end he knew that his Inventor is the sole author and architect of his potential, not the world, so despite these words, he continued to study and improve himself. Some thirty odd years or so later, P was invited overseas to speak, where he began selling and signing his books after his speaking engagements. On one such occasion, he noticed a very old man, who had patiently stood in line and waited his turn, coming towards him to get his book signed. P noticed that the old man's book was quite old and looked 'used', meaning he had bought it a while ago. With his walking stick, he proceeded to the table, sat down and presented his book. After his book was signed, instead of standing up to allow the next person to sit and get their book signed, the old man remained seated and did not budge. So P asked if there was anything wrong, for he did not recognise him. The old man shook his head and said there was nothing wrong. So they stared at each other for a while, P gradually feeling a bit awkward and uncomfortable, until the old man, now with tears running down his cheeks, asked, "You don't recognise me, do you?" and P replied, "No Sir, unfortunately not". The old man then went on to explain who he was and when he realised that he was his former teacher, both of them began to embrace, laughing and crying at the same time. The old man began to profusely apologise and express deep regret over what he had said and the pain he had caused, begging for forgiveness. Tearfully, he added that over the years he had read his former student's books and that they had made such a profound difference in his life. After being reassured that forgiveness was his and that it had been for a very long time, they happily parted ways. The old man passed away not too long after that. Had P believed his teachers' words about him and made them his reality, chances are he would have never even scratched the surface of his life's accomplishments.

Granted, it is true that we live in a world of labels. These days we have a label for everything and that is okay - for the most part. The problem arises when we want to label people. Labels should be restricted to things or objects, not people. We even label ourselves and somehow adjust to and live by our self-imposed labels. Interestingly, once you label yourself, all the limitations of those labels apply to you. There are labels which are acceptable because of their administrative nature; that is, they bring order and ensure the smooth running of life's activities. Examples are our names and surnames. It would be impractical and ineffective to live life without them, short of just reducing people to numbers. Still, even those numbers would be for management purposes. Other labels have to do with our careers, i.e. doctor, dancer, teacher, engineer, CEO, chairperson, etc. Others have to do with our current situation or status, like, addict or recovering addict, wealthy, pauper, infertile, childless, black, white, tall, short, beautiful, ugly, inmate, student, etc. The problem is people start to see and treat each other according to society's view on that particular label, sometimes to such an extent that the individual eventually also begins to see themselves in that light. Let us not forget that labelling is a choice and as such, we need to separate people from them. Simply put, labels are just other people's opinion of you. You and I are human beings before we are our names and surnames, diseases, teachers, doctors, addicts, failures, successes and the rest. The truth is that we never really choose our labels. They mostly stem from things such as culture, background, religion, race, families and past experiences. Remember that opinions are not the truth, in the sense that they do not and cannot capture the wholeness of who you are, so you need to choose what **you** will believe for yourself – either who your Inventor says you are or people's opinion of you. It took me quite a while to come to the realisation that I actually do have the power to choose what I will believe because I had mostly thought that public opinion was paramount. A few years into my marriage we still could not conceive, so I was labelled infertile and childless. I lived through stares of pity and shame, endured callous and insensitive comments, lost some friends and gained new ones and enjoyed the love and support of family – all in one experience. At first, I took the persona of the labels and saw myself through the eyes of society. I defined myself by my circumstances, hating myself in the process. I was so depressed I became suicidal... All over something I could not control. Imagine that! Not only was I not valued by society but I also did not value myself, so much so that I was considering taking my own life because of this one thing. I did not realise that there is so much more to me than my circumstances; that my value supersedes any label or condition. I eventually began to understand and appreciate that any label that undermines my value as a human being, is not something I should be wasting my time on entertaining. My purpose is far greater than the hurdles I must manoeuvre to get there. I finally realised that I am actually a whole complete being, full of untapped potential, neither defined by nor limited to my circumstances. I realised I am here for a reason and that my assignment can only be uniquely fulfilled by me; that humanity will be better off because I am here. I am a creator of fact and not a creature of circumstance. The truth is you cannot please everybody, hard as you may try - people's opinions are too transitory, that you can believe; but your Creator's opinion of you will not change, no matter what! People's opinions will say many different and often contradicting things like, "Oh, it's such a pity you can't have babies of your own" or "What, three children?...that's too much!" or "They need to just put a sock in it now" or "Why have they waited so long to have a child?" or "Why do they only have one child, they need to have at least one or two more?" and so on, even to the point of being told that you are just lazy, that is why it is taking longer than usual... the list is endless. These are just some of the statements I have heard. It then proves futile to allow opinions, be they self-imposed or other people's, to be the standard in your life, unless or until they attest to your value.

Allow me to illustrate with this example. There was once an army general who sent out a group of soldiers to go and spy on land that they believed they were to occupy. The aim was to see what there was and possibly do a SWOT analysis (that is, identify Strengths, Weaknesses, Opportunities and Threats), which could then assist them with the planning of how to occupy the land. So the spies prepared themselves and began the journey to fulfil their assignment. They were also asked to do their best to bring back some produce from the land. A few weeks later the spies returned and gave their report to the army general. As they presented the fruit they had picked, they went on to say that they found the land rich, fertile and desirable. Just as the army general was getting ready to take possession of the land and conquer it, some of the spies in the group began to sing another song. They strongly advised that it would be unwise to move forward because they saw giants that were too strong for them, explaining that they felt as small as grasshoppers in their eyes; they believed that is exactly how they must have looked to 'the giants'.

Does this story sound familiar to some of us? Here are some observations I made from this story:

1. They may have started off feeling strong and well able to 'grab life by the horns' when they left but they came back feeling defeated because of what they thought they saw.

2. Even with all the positive experiences of the rich, fertile and desirable land, they managed to see something they believe to be a hindrance, that is, the giant-looking people.

3. They then made a conclusion that would affect not only that current time but also have an effect going forward. Due to what they thought they saw, they wrote-off any attempt at occupying the land as planned.

So we see here that labels that are outside the boundary of the product's user manual are quite dangerous, even those that are self-imposed. They produce dysfunction because they cause you to function outside of your purpose. Even amidst positive things, one can find something negative and make that their focal point. In this case, the spies 'saw themselves' as grasshoppers, not the people of the land and because that was their self-concept, they then believed that was how the people viewed them. How tragic is that? That is how they saw themselves, so they projected that to the people of the land. I believe that anytime we perceive someone or something as a giant, we probably feel in one way or the other that we are smaller in comparison. The reason why you would believe people see you a certain way is that you already believe that about yourself – you see yourself that way first and then believe that others see the same.

When we choose to believe these labels, whether positive or negative, we begin to see ourselves in that light. Then we go through life, situation after situation, seeing ourselves and even our future that way. You cannot and should not define yourself by your circumstances, because you are not them. They are transitory by nature and therefore a variable. Can you honestly imagine yourself being many different variables at once? I'm sure it would feel like being tossed all over, like clothing in a washing machine. Today you are this and tomorrow that. The question you should ask yourself is: whilst you are busy being those variables, who is being you…the real you? Are you not depriving yourself and humanity as a whole of the precious gem that you are, of the rich potential that already exists in you? This puts a responsibility on you to guard your thoughts about yourself because they will not only reflect on you but also on others. Along with our purpose comes the freedom to choose. This is how we differ from animals and objects. Our Creator gave us an added special gift - the freedom of choice. Lifeless things or objects like dry leaves that have fallen off a tree are swept up by the wind and they are sent to any and all directions the wind chooses and that is okay; those things are just that…things or objects. They are lifeless and therefore have no will against the wind in this example. The human person, on the other hand, is primarily a spiritual being who possesses and enjoys both freedom and responsibility. This unique quality enables and empowers the human to rise above their circumstances and overcome them, instead of being overcome by their circumstances.

Who you are is constant. It does not change. **No one else qualifies to be you but you – so live your best life now!** I dare you to ask anyone who has ever invented anything, **there is no greater pleasure for a manufacturer than to witness his invention**

become what he created it to be and to manifest all the potential it carries. The same applies to our Creator.

CHAPTER 2

You Are Not Your Best Achievements or Possessions

WE SHOULD ALWAYS KEEP OUR BEHAVIOUR OR PERFORMANCE SEPARATE FROM OUR SENSE OF SELF-WORTH

~ MYLES MUNROE

For me, the subject of purpose and its role in human behaviour is not only important but also quite interesting. I can personally attest to life having more meaning and fulfilment when I am working towards a specific goal at any given time, compared to when I am idle and aimless. When I am working towards a goal, three things happen. First, I feel a sense of significance like I am an important individual just because the goal is there, daring me to act; waiting for me to do something about it. It means that I can actually achieve it. Secondly, I feel a sense of pride and contentedness when the goal is attained and that is such a good feeling. Thirdly, it invokes in me the desire to achieve more. In other words, one sense of accomplishment begs for another, simply because of the belief that it can be done and also because of the effect it has on its recipients. So if achieving a certain goal improves the quality of life for a group of people, for instance, then I would most likely be inspired to attain more of the same goals.

As virtuous as that may sound, sadly, it does not always remain that way, at least not in the long run. Often we 'miss the point' after a while and begin to focus on the feelings of significance, the pride and the euphoria that comes with attaining a goal. While these things are not wrong, shifting the focus from the goal, purpose or assignment to the euphoria can impede your virtuous journey. The way I see it, this is a cause and effect relationship. **A cause and effect** relationship is a relationship in which one event (the cause) makes another event happen (the effect). All the experiences mentioned above (the significance, pride, euphoria, etc.) come about as a result of the pursuit of purpose or meaning. Simply put, your purpose is the **cause** and the result thereafter is the **effect**. When we start to focus on the effect and make that our comfort zone, we miss the point completely because the cause not only **guarantees the effect** but also **sustains it**. The effect may come in different forms, for example, wealth, riches, status, fame, happiness, possessions, success, joy, etc., all of which are the result of a cause. How fleeting then is the effect without the cause, how meaningless! Indeed, if the existence of the effect is solely dependent on the cause, how meaningless is the effect without the cause. In other words, **the meaning is in the cause** and not the effect.

I like Viktor Frankl's take on cause and effect. He says:

"Don't aim at success – the more you aim at it and make it a target, the more you are going to miss it. For success, like happiness, cannot be pursued; it must ensue and it only does so as the unintended side effect of one's dedication to a course greater than oneself or as the by-product of one's surrender to a person other than oneself. Happiness must happen and the same holds for success: you have to let it happen by not caring about it"

As well as:

"Life is not primarily a quest for pleasure, as Freud believed or a quest for power, as Alfred Alder taught, but a quest for meaning. The great task for any person is to find meaning in his or her life".

As we humans have been created for a cause, how does it become logical to define ourselves according to the effect, focusing on it to such an extent that the cause slowly but surely dissipates into oblivion? Then when the effect runs its course and fades because there is no course to sustain it, we crash with it – and what a massive thud that can be. This is because we have identified ourselves with what is now basically non-existent due to its transient nature, so that is exactly how we will feel, empty. Ouch! Myles Munroe says, "He who gets his personal worth from the things he possesses must be sure to never lose his possessions"; and "Our value and self-worth derive from who we are, not what we have". In my opinion, trying to find one's identity in the effect is both futile and dangerous because it's a set up for a life of disappointments.

Let us further explore this by looking into the lives of those who pursue the cause and those who pursue the effect.

Cause Pursuers

1. Are not in danger of falling into an existential vacuum or experience inner emptiness, which is mostly characterised by boredom.

2. Are driven because they have a goal to achieve.

3. Use their time wisely and maximise their potential because they know that they are responsible for fulfilling or attaining a goal.

4. Are focused and they carefully choose the company they keep because they do not want to enable distractions and delays to their mission.

5. The satisfaction or self-actualisation that comes with achieving the goal makes them want to do more and so permanently distance themselves from the danger of 'boredom'.

6. Because of their purpose-driven nature, they have a reason to be happy when that purpose is attained.

7. Do not pursue happiness but happiness follows them when they fulfil their purpose.

8. Pleasure or happiness is not the goal of cause pursuers but only a side effect of attaining a goal; attaining the goal constitutes a reason to be joyful.

Effect Pursuers

1. Are prone to experiencing an existential vacuum (inner emptiness) because, like a drug fix for example, once the

drugs wear out and the thrill is gone, the massive thud ensues and depression may eventually set in.

2. Are self-defeating. The more they aim at the effect, the more they miss it, like chasing after a mirage of water in the desert.

3. Are not likely to respect or use their time wisely.

4. Because man is wired to strive towards and fulfil a goal, intentionally failing to do so may result in being bored and the boredom by-products ensue - which is more often than not, a lot of trouble.

5. They self-actualise, meaning they are only concerned with fulfilment of self rather than meaning, which if made an effect in itself, contradicts the self-transcendent quality of human existence.

It was never in the plan of the Creator for man to be mastered by things. On the contrary, His plan was that man should be the master of things. Genesis 1:28, "Then God blessed them and God said to them, 'Be fruitful and multiply; fill the earth and subdue it; have dominion over the fish of the sea, over the birds of the air and over every living thing that [b]moves on the earth'".

We must dominate, meaning to rule, to manage, to govern and to control things but **not** to be ruled and controlled by them. According to this instruction, we are also not to dominate each other. It does not say, "Have dominion over one another". That is why people retaliate when being controlled and subdued. It could take a while but retaliation is inevitable, simply because man was not created to rule over other people; only things. So based on this truth, the conclusion I come to is that the only worthy thing to be mastered by or be a slave to is your gift, potential and assignment - **not** things!

Most times we think that our greatest test is when we go through difficult times but the truth is the test is there even in times of blessing. The general pattern is that once blessing comes, complacency creeps in. I have seen people who start off in humble circumstances, change and become something else. They become strangely different when they come into a blessing. Some people, who had been committed members before, either reduce attendance or stop going to church completely after securing a job – because now they are too busy. Yet others will change their values and compromise their conviction in order to 'fit' in and be accepted at certain groups that they feel will enhance their perceived success. Needless to say, these decisions usually adversely affect a lot of people around them and have unpleasant effects. For example, you suddenly find yourself with more money than you ever had. As a result, you may start to feel like you are 'better' or 'higher' than other people who have less than you do; and therefore start treating them like they are beneath you because that is how you now see them. These could be family or friends but you have changed how you see them in an instant, all because of a fugacious situation. Now, you have not only labelled and defined yourself by your circumstances but you have gone ahead and done the same to other people. The question we should all be asking ourselves here is: what happens when the circumstances change or become obsolete? What then? Will you now change and label or define yourself differently? If your circumstances change for the worst, for example, how will you label and define yourself and other people? I think we can agree that this would be too much administration, wouldn't it! It definitely would not leave any room for fun, to be yourself and to enjoy who you really are, because the truth is, who you are is to be explored and enjoyed to the fullest. When you do that, then the rest of humanity can benefit from the authentic gift that you are. You are not things and things are not you. Your circumstances are here today and gone tomorrow, so they cannot and should not define who you are. Do not allow them to! I figure the best way to live an uncomplicated life is to see yourself and other people as they are, not through the clouded lenses of what they have or lack, what they have done, their status, race, physique, etc. In other words, reduce everyone to a human being and life will become less and less of a mystery to you. Always remember that **what you do in your moment of blessing actually determines how significant your next season will become.** Can you be trusted with more or must the little that you have be taken from you because of how you conduct yourself?

We are not entrusted with things to make other people's lives worse than they are but so their lives may be enhanced. Life is far more important than things because while we do not need things to have life, we do need life to have things. All these gifts, talents and things that our Inventor entrusts us with are not to make us important. He gives them to us because we **are** important! So please do not do your Inventor and yourself an injustice by attaching your already established and potent importance to something so small and fleeting. Do not make light of who you really are. Doing this will cause dysfunction. The word dysfunction means a disruption of normal social relations or an impairment in the operation of an organ or system. You and I are built to function a certain way and we have been endowed with everything we could ever need to function that way. This means that anytime we allow things that could hamper or compromise how we should function, we create dysfunction. We could be so comfortable with the dysfunction that we even go to the extent of giving it a name, which then gives it credence. For example, there are many different groups of people in the world today, from different societal backgrounds. For the longest time we have heard stories of how one group would perceive themselves as greater, purer, more intelligent and more entitled than others. Often, they will attempt to annihilate the perceived 'lower' group, calling it cleansing or purging humanity and the earth. In so doing, they have given a virtuous name to a dysfunction and sadly, any time we do that we not only legitimise the dysfunction but we also give it the power to increase. This is a dysfunction because from what we have learnt so far, every human person is equally important and deeply valuable because of their unique purpose and role that they are to play in this life. **We all have the potential to lead and excel in our different areas of gifting**. We may be different but that does not mean we are better than the next person. In fact, what becomes evident is how much we need each other and that we should only strive to be better - not when compared to each other but better at our assignment. So, no one, nor a group of people, can be better than others in their areas of gifting and there are no gifts that are below or above others, all are equally important according to the Creator and everyone comes well-equipped to function in their gift.

Granted, we all need to be affirmed and celebrated but that celebration that another person gives you is not a cause, it is just an effect. Do not be tempted to think it is the cause and allow it to define you. People's opinions generally change. You may be celebrated and affirmed in the morning and by late afternoon, that opinion of you has changed. The point here is to keep on growing, doing and being more and more in your assignment. You have that potential and capacity. Imagine a person coming back from work in the evening and looking forward to a hearty meal – but when the food comes, they get more excited by the spices and other condiments, rather than the meal itself. The affirmations would be the spices, not the main meal; make sure you keep your focus on the meal and not the spices. Yes, the spices are an important part of the meal because they add flavour to it but that does not make them the meal, it makes them **part** of the meal. So if you prioritise people's opinion, your achievements and possessions, until it becomes the basis for your identity, you are in trouble because it will not satisfy you.

CHAPTER 3

You Are Not Your Feelings or Failures

NEVER MAKE A PERMANENT DECISION BASED ON A TEMPORARY SITUATION

~ MYLES MUNROE

Normally, things or situations make us 'feel' a certain way; and situations change all the time, some more rapidly and drastically than others. Consequently, by allowing our emotions to be swayed back and forth like a pendulum, we find ourselves constantly being unsettled and anxious. Where there is worry there is no faith and where there is no faith there is despair. Where despair abounds, you become a sitting duck for the currents of life to carry you anywhere and everywhere. Since situations change, it follows that the resulting feelings will change too, because they are a by-product of the situation. For example, you may feel a certain way about a friend who you thought said something bad about you, only to find that they did not say what you think they said. A while later after they explain everything, your feelings towards them may change. Feelings come and go, depending on the information that we receive and choose to accept. While feeling in itself is not wrong, it is how we react to or how we process those feelings that can be detrimental to our wellbeing. Allowing your feelings to define who you are is nothing short of heinous to who you really could be. We may feel a certain way, yes but that does not mean we are what we feel. When you are feeling angry, that doesn't make you the anger. When you are sad, you are not the sadness. You are experiencing a moment of sadness. To remove yourself from the feeling – do not own it. This will help protect you from making permanent decisions based on temporary situations.

I will be honest and admit that most of the decisions I have ever regretted making were ones I made in the heat of the moment, that is, in anger, hurt, disappointment or fear. These decisions usually carry long-lasting and undesirable effects; all because I did not separate myself from those feelings. They even have the ability to destroy not just your life but the lives of other people too. It is both amazing and unfortunate how a lifetime can be affected by a brief moment.

Feelings are just things that happen as a result of our everyday experiences and they only take the meaning that we give to those experiences. Life is made up of many different moments and it is the meaning that we give to those unique moments that eventually determines how our lifetime is affected. Sadly, in the times we are living in today, most of us are governed by feelings, in our leadership, parenting, in the classroom, the boardroom, our marriages and other relationships - the consequences of which are often dire, to say the least. That being said, it would be impractical for me not to acknowledge that separating oneself from one's feelings is easier said than done. Maybe it can be done, one moment, one experience at a time; and can then be perfected over time. There is a difference between doing the right thing and doing what you 'feel' like doing. Doing the right thing for a particular moment is like obeying a law. Law is just that... Law! It does not discriminate, it does not take sides, it has no mood swings, it does not change colour, it does not change to accommodate the seasons...IT JUST IS! The law requires that you obey it whether you feel like it or not. Your feelings about it are not more important than you aligning yourself with it and if you contravene the law, there are explicit consequences. So, for example, when I stop at a stop sign, it is not always because I 'feel' good about it...sometimes I am really in a hurry and would really like to just scurry on. I have to stop not only because of the immediate consequences of a possible ticket or fine but also more so, those of even bigger magnitude, i.e. running a stop sign could cause a collision with another motorist who has the right of way. And there you have it – my brief moment of impatience and anxiety could adversely affect the life of one or even more people. We do not do the right thing because we feel like it; no! We do the right thing because it is our responsibility to do so.

So when you remove yourself from your feelings you not only protect yourself from adverse consequences but you unwittingly do the same for others as well. Another example could be a person who wants to lose weight. The law, in this case, could be that, in addition to eating a healthy diet, they must 'hit the gym' in the morning before going to work and maybe even after work, depending on the gravity of the situation. When the clock strikes at 5 am, what are the chances that this person always 'feels' good and is excited about waking up and going to the gym? Probably close to none - yet when they separate themselves from their feelings and focus on the goal, they become more aware of their responsibility and they wake up and do the right thing at that moment. I must say this is what gets me on the road in the morning – focusing on the goal and being reminded of my responsibility towards my health at that moment; not my feelings. If I went along with how I feel about it, I probably would not do it at all.

Here are some suggestions on how to separate yourself from your feelings:

1. **Know who you are.** This will help you to also know who you are not – your feelings.

2. **Be aware that choice is available to you.** Your feelings cannot and should not deprive you of your right to choose. Be confident that you can choose responsibility over your feelings.

3. **Recognise that moment as unique to you.** Do not try to compare it with other people's similar experiences. That way your experience, the choices you make and ultimately the meaning you give to that moment will only be unique to you.

4. **Take responsibility for the choices you make.** Your choices should be ones that if required, you can stand up for, back up and not shy away from.

5. **Consider the welfare of others.** Are the choices that you make going to be of help and benefit other people or not? Remember the stop sign example?

Show me a life ruled by feelings and I will show you a life that is mostly filled with pain and regret.

One of the most feared possibilities in life is failure. Again, failure is just an experience; it does not become the person who is experiencing it. So failure and a person are two different things. Owning it and identifying yourself with it gives a distorted view of yourself. I believe that every moment in life, whether pleasant or not, presents us with something to take away. Failure, just like feelings, is a very real part of life but more importantly, it is just as transient. It is just a 'brief moment' in our life and as such, we cannot afford to let it define a whole lifetime. You know in a way, failure is almost necessary, because it is what prepares us for success, depending on how we react to it. If we fail once and remain there, then the failure remains. However, if we keep on rising every time we fall and try again, success cannot elude us for much longer. *Tom Krause* says, "There are no failures--just experiences and your reactions to them" and Maya Angelou says, "History, despite its wrenching pain, cannot be unlived but if faced with courage, need not be lived again". Sometimes we can view our physical impediments, such as a lisp or a limp, as failure and as a result, refrain from answering to our calling because we feel, "Oh what's the point, I'll never be able to do it perfectly or like so-and-so because I cannot speak or walk like them".

There was once a man who was really good with electronics and over the years had created a few gadgets that could do things for him, like run errands, store information, schedule and remind him of appointments, etc. Even though he was quite fond of his creation, the man was lonely and he yearned for a companion he could relate to at a more personal or more human level. So he went about learning more and challenging himself, eventually perfecting his skill to the point where he felt ready to try his technological breakthrough. He began the arduous and intricate process of creating that companion that he so longed for. After a few stints of trial and error, he finally found himself beholding his object of desire. As he continued to gaze at it, he realised for the first time how different it was from the rest of his creations. He proudly recalled that this was due to the fact that this time around, he had added his own characteristics and traits into the mix. So this one, whom he called BOTMAN Version 2.0, was able to reason, ask basic questions, provide answers when asked to, and display the rudiments of human emotion. The creator suddenly realised why the process had been so arduous and complicated – he was doing something he had never done before; he was creating from his whole being, not just from his head. He realised that he had literally 'poured' a tinge of his essence into BOTMAN Version 2.0, thus the difference to the others and the special connection. BOTMAN could do what the other gadgets could do and then some. One of his special features was that he could display words on a screen located on his chest area as though in conversation. This is how he was programmed to answer questions; as his creator had not yet perfected his speaking ability, so his spoken vocabulary was too limited to sustain a simple conversation.

One day, the creator discovered a potential threat. It came to his attention that a man known as Rofa was attempting to replicate his creation, retain the ownership rights and profit from it. This discovery came at a time when he was right in the middle of another project that he could not take time away from. After a few telephone conversations which proved futile because Rofa had dug his heels in and refused to back down. They finally resorted to meet in person. Since the creator could not go himself, he entrusted this meeting to BOTMAN, because he knew that he had equipped him with all he would need to stand in for him at the meeting. You can imagine his surprise when BOTMAN gave him all sorts of excuses to justify not going to the meeting. The creator tried to explain over and over again, to the point of becoming irate, that he is the one that created BOTMAN and therefore he is the one who knew what BOTMAN could do and not do; and that BOTMAN could do this. The main excuse that BOTMAN gave was that he did not have enough vocabulary to speak and he had to speak and not display words because he was going to meet with someone who speaks. BOTMAN felt he could not answer this calling because he could not communicate the way he thought he should and yet he could communicate the way his creator had programmed him to. Can you see the difference? If BOTMAN were to move his focus from his perceived weakness of not being able to communicate by speaking and concentrate on his gift of being able to communicate through his screen (chest), he would be able to maximise his potential.

I have discovered that the weakness you see in yourself may actually be your strong point because it is through that weakness that you can eventually discover your strengths. Sounds weird I know, but not so much when you think about it. It's like having many options that don't work at your disposal and out of sheer frustration, you eventually do everything in your power to find one that works. So, to learn a valuable lesson from BOTMAN, we must apply the principle of not defining or identifying ourselves by our failures or the feelings we experience, or even our perceived weaknesses. Our inability to see ourselves separate from feelings and failure could have repercussions which include the following:

1. **Unrealised potential.** Many people live and eventually meet their death without releasing and maximising their potential. The reasons they would give include, fear of failure, no opportunities, no resources, physical limitations, their past, level of education - the list is endless. Even more unfortunate is when it affects other people as well. So, by not realising your potential, someone else's potential might not be realised. It's now not just about you, but about others as well. If my son's music teacher had not bothered to study music for whatever reason, he would not be teaching my son now; if he was not teaching him, my son, even though he loves music, would not be harnessing his gift. On the other side of your obedience to your calling, someone's breakthrough awaits. Discover who you are so others can discover who they are.

2. **Dependence on past experience.** You are most likely to use what felt good to you and your perceived successes as a reference point. You may feel you can do it because you have done it before. However, you are only limiting yourself to that known experience and you're not giving yourself the opportunity to experience more through your untapped potential.

3. **Stuck in a rut.** I believe one of the default settings that human beings enjoy is growth in its entirety. That is why

we are always striving towards something more and always searching for more. Man is always caught between what is and what should be and reaching towards what should be necessitates growth. That growth may not always be comfortable or a welcome change but it is necessary nonetheless. If we are not growing we may start to feel frustrated, as though we are stuck in a rut. Johnathan Tropper is quoted as saying, "The only difference between a rut and a grave is depth". Short of one being deeper than the other, they are basically the same. My interpretation is that if you entertain being in a rut long enough, it will become a grave. The truth is, there is a high possibility that most of us will, at some point, find ourselves in a rut and that is okay; as long as we make it as short a visit as possible, otherwise the grave looms. This means that the absence of growth implies death. Parents become worried when their baby faces developmental challenges which stunt their growth. That is because growth is a necessity for humans. So, allowing past experiences (whether good or bad) or your feelings to define you, instead of answering to your calling and realising the rich potential it comes with, will definitely make you feel like you are trapped in a rut because there can be no growth there. The past is not there to define us and keep us with it, it is there for us to grow and learn from; to use those lessons to cultivate a better future. If perceived with the right attitude, the past can very well act as a catalyst for growth.

4. **Hopelessness.** Hopelessness sets in when you start doubting that life has meaning and that you exist for a reason and therefore you matter. Being stuck in a rut long

enough will do that to you. I believe the psychological term for this is an existential vacuum. Our feelings and failures are just events in our existence. They are not carved in stone; they change all the time so we cannot afford to make them the compass that directs the continuation of our life. We can learn from them but that's about all.

Every product has and can reach an optimal level of function; only when it is functioning within its purpose, does it realise and maximise its potential. The same applies to us. Some people will tell you how they are at their happiest when they do something they love. For them, at that moment, things like failure, disappointment, sadness, depression, etc., are the least of their concerns. Simply put, do not try to find your assignment by what you think you are good at; find it by what you have been called to do. This way you have access to any and every gift you need to fulfil the assignment. However, if you try to find your assignment by only what you think you are good at and your experiences, you are limiting yourself to only what you already know. Sadly, that is all you will have access to. What about all the other things and possibilities that you have not yet experienced, let alone imagined? There will always be something more for you to learn, discover and explore. Such is the gift that we have been given – which is life. I know that while my feelings and experiences may change, the potential and resources I have to answer my calling never will. I will always have unlimited access to them in every moment. This epiphany has led me to this conclusion: you cannot change your assignment to fit what you feel good about. There may be times when you feel you are not doing a good job at fulfilling your assignment, you may even feel like you 'stink' at it but that does not give you the right to change it. It did not come from you, so you have no right to alter it. Why? It is not about what you like or feel good about, it is about your calling. We often make this mistake: what I'm good at first, then my assignment. Wrong! It's your assignment first, then your gift, because your **gift is the provision for the assignment!**

WHO YOU ARE

CHAPTER 4

You Are Your Source

All things produce after themselves. Humans produce humans, different plants produce plants in their likeness, and different animals produce animals in their likeness too. Producing after oneself is a very serious and involved process; it is not just a distant and meaningless process. You cannot just sit and be a spectator when producing after yourself – your involvement is such that you literally have to share a part of yourself to make it possible. We often exclaim at the uncanny resemblance of a son to his dad or of a daughter to her mother. This is because in as much as both parents are human, they do not just produce any human…but one that is specific to them in every way; one which they literally must share a part of themselves with to make up who they are. This is known as passing on ones' genes to the next generation. The child can take this further and adopt his/her parents' personality and be outgoing, business-minded or even artistic, for example. From this, we can deduce that all things have the same components and essence as their source.

You and I have the same components and essence as our Creator too. Yes, God created the plants, animals and indeed humans too; but man is different in that he lives in three dimensions: the somatic, the mental and the spiritual. It is through this spiritual dimension that we are able to relate with our Creator. In the story of creation, it is of particular interest to note that whatever God spoke to became the source from which the created thing came. In Genesis 1:3-25, God is talking to things to bring forth things from themselves. When He brought forth the stars, He spoke to the firmament; for the fish He spoke to the water and for the plants and animals, He spoke to the earth. But then something totally different and very significant happened next. Verse 26-28 says:

> "Then God said, 'Let Us make man in Our image, according to Our likeness; let them have dominion over the fish of the sea, over the birds of the air and over the cattle, over[g] all the earth and over every creeping thing that creeps on the earth'. 27 So God created man in His own image; in the image of God He created him; male and female He created them. 28 Then God blessed them and God said to them, 'Be fruitful and multiply; fill the earth and subdue it; **have dominion** over the fish of the sea, over the birds of the air and over every living thing that[h] moves on the earth."

When God was getting ready to bring forth His best, what did He do? He probably came to the conclusion that speaking to things was not good enough because those things would not be able to produce the exact calibre and quality of His ultimate creation.

So He went into consultation and convened a meeting with the ultimate for His ultimate creation – that is, **He spoke to Himself!** How amazing is that? He called a meeting and consulted with Himself / the Trinity – yes, you and I are that important! He created you and me out of Himself and for Himself – in other words, He poured Himself out by literally taking out a part of himself to make you and me possible. Imagine for a moment that you are holding a pitcher that has liquid in it. Now imagine pouring out that same liquid from the pitcher into an empty glass. Compare the two liquids and see if there is any difference. I can tell you now there will not be. You will find that the liquid in the glass is exactly the same in essence and components to the one in the pitcher. This is exactly how we were created. When it came to the human, our Creator poured Himself out and endowed us with His image and likeness, meaning we resemble and function like Him. God elevated man above all His creations by making man share in his image and likeness, which again shows the superiority of man over all creation.

The Hebrew word for image is 'selem', meaning 'essential nature'. It implies not looking alike but being alike. The Hebrew word for likeness is 'demuth', meaning characteristics, traits, potential or function. In other words, man has a brain with a spirit that gives him an identity, free will, the ability to think and plan ahead like God, the ability to appreciate the value and responsibility to make choices. It is this factor that contains man's ultimate true potential. We are made to reflect the personhood of our Creator. In other words, we have His character and authority to dominate, as per the mandate above. The word 'dominate' again means to rule, manage, control (keep under control), subject, influence, lead, govern, command, master and to have authority and power over.

In the verses above lies not only the purpose for your creation but also your nature because whatever God creates He also gives it the nature to produce its purpose. Please note that the mandate is very specific about what we are to dominate and those specifics do not include other humans. Human beings were never meant to be dominated, regardless of their colour, creed, sex, status, position, education level, etc. We know from history that any attempt to do so inevitably leads to rebellion and usually ends in disaster. This is simply because no human was meant to be dominated by another. The dominion is over things, **not** over people. Even children sometimes rebel when they feel they don't like or agree with what you are saying. If then we resemble and function like Him, we too have His authority, character, moral and spiritual nature to dominate in our different areas of influence according to the gifts and talents He gives us to produce our purpose. You come already wired for your purpose. Your race, physical features, birth - everything about you is related to it. You are perfect and enough for your assignment! That is why prioritising other people's opinions (and even your own opinion) of yourself above your Creators' is both unfortunate and self-defeating. It undermines your potential. The truth is **you really don't have to do anything extra to qualify to be you**. God did not wait for or expect a certain action or performance from you before determining your value…He just did! So why would you let your behaviour or performance determine your self-worth? Your value was determined long before you existed and the best part is that it came free from terms and conditions. Wow! How about that? This tells me that according to your manufacturer, there is nothing that you can do or not do, that would make you any less valuable to Him. There is nothing that would make Him think less of you.

Simply put, when God said, "Let us make man in our image and likeness", He was declaring the end from the beginning. He was making you perfect and complete long before you manifested physically. Do you think at that stage He didn't know that you would err sometimes, make bad decisions, indulge in wicked behaviour, fail, get discouraged, give up or even face extremely difficult situations; no! I mean if you think about it, while man has used his ability to think and create for good, he has also used it to create weapons of mass destruction and has used his knowledge of the human body to create poisons that kill people. Others have used creation to perform all kinds of witchcraft and black magic. Man has even taken something good like sex and created something evil like rape and prostitution. Even though all this was not hidden from Him, He still declared your perfect end from the beginning.

Could it be that the Creator's plan was never for man to be aware of eventualities but rather to be aware of Him as the source? I am convinced this is the case; for to be constantly more aware of Him is to come closer and closer to His image and likeness. You see, making these eventualities a focal point compartmentalises mankind; it makes some either superior or inferior to the other, whether by education, position, race, rank, status, sex, etc., which then leads to man dominating each other. There is always more to man than his eventualities. **What you see with your eyes is not all there is to life.** The former president of South Africa, Nelson Mandela, was sent to prison for 27 years and those who incarcerated him probably just saw a criminal, terrorist and a "useless" black man; and yet inside of him was the president of a nation of over 40 million people. The colour of his skin and being imprisoned were just events in his life; but inside of him was a free man, a president! History has more examples of such people and my point again is that there is more to man than his eventualities. The world can and probably will try to label you and keep you confined in that box but it cannot touch or destroy the authentic being that you are on the inside…the original wonder of your Creator. I say this because after He created you, He beheld you and couldn't help but admit to Himself that He was a genius. Genesis 1:31(a) says, "Then God saw everything that He had made and indeed it was very good". God saw all He had created as very good. This is because He knew what He had placed in man. He knew man's value and worth, which was not in man's eventualities. There is something wonderful, pure and genuine about relating to someone based on their inward value than their supposed outward value.

Declaring the end from the beginning is especially intriguing to me because it tells me that there is something that He gave me that qualifies me to be who He says I am and that is not subject to the events and situations in my life; it just is. This is what I call your authentic value. The definition of value in this context is the regard that someone is held to deserve; the importance, worth or usefulness of someone. Clearly, your Creator places your value way above life's eventualities and if He can see the value in you, then you can see it in yourself; and if you can see it in yourself, then you can surely see it in others. I believe that is the key right there. We relate differently to people when we value them, as opposed to when we don't. I contend that every atrocity that man has faced, be it slavery, racial discrimination, xenophobia, sexual abuse, emotional abuse, physical abuse, or any other form of subjugation, is not the result of the **absence of value** but rather the **ignorance of value**. Don't fall into the trap of mistaking the two. In the unfortunate event that someone mistreats you or has low or no regard for you, don't think it's because you have no value; it is because they don't see it. It is not your fault either, because you cannot be responsible for people's blindness, can you? Nope, I don't think so! Now the benefit of knowing your own value is that you are then able to erect boundaries that let people know how to treat you and how not to. Don't we always protect and preserve the things we value? For example, our material possessions; we even go to the extent of insuring them and locking them up in safes. When you value people you will perceive and treat them according to that value and not according to their circumstances!

One of the greatest attributes of man is his freedom to choose; but having said that, I must also emphasise that this freedom of choice comes with responsibility. We are all free to choose and make our own decisions but we need to make them responsibly. No one, not even your Creator can force you to make a choice that you don't want to make, that is why He gave you the freedom to choose. Yes, there is the matter of consequences for all decisions and subsequent actions but the consequences (especially for the bad decisions) are meant as a corrective measure to help change you for the better; they do not change your value. There is something about knowing not just who you are but taking it further to discover why you are, then acting on it. For example, it's not enough for a car to know that it is a car. It also needs to understand its function, which is to provide transport. Otherwise, it could be content just parked in the garage or under a tree until it rusts and wears away into nothing. In this example, the car discovering its purpose gives it not only its value but also the authority to be on the road and do what it needs to do. Likewise, your purpose not only comes with potential but also gives you the authority to pursue it. True authority is the authority to operate in ones' gifts and talents to fulfil ones' purpose. That is how we are able to dominate the earth. This authority can be likened to that of a police officer. A police officer only has the authority to stop and inspect cars on the road when he is in full uniform and wearing a badge. If he stops you, you are compelled by the law to stop. His or her race, physical stature or financial status really don't matter, in fact very little matters at that time, except his full authority that is backed by the government to stop you if necessary for your safety and that of other citizens. Whether you like it or not, you must slow down and stop. That is the authority the officer has. Note that the same officer also has value. We realise this value when we feel threatened and in need of protection. I have heard people talk about how they had never been happier and so relieved to see a police officer when they felt unsafe. The value of the officer is in his function – which is to protect. Now let's take the same officer and remove his uniform and badge, making him a civilian. Say he then stands on the highway and tries to stop cars without the authority to do so. What do you think would happen? I think he would more than likely be run over. Most people would not give him the time of day because as a mere civilian, he does not have the authority to compel motorists to stop. Also, as a civilian, his value to protect may be slightly undermined, because he will not have legal access to the tools and means to protect you at the time. So, your purpose gives you legal access and authority to everything you need to fulfil it. You have access to all the places you need to be at and the people you are to meet to fulfil your purpose.

Your purpose also comes packed with its provision. If your purpose is to take you to point C from point A, via point D, don't try to get there via point B. The reason is that the point B route may not have the provision you will need, because it was not in the plan in the first place. Or, it may be a provision that is not suitable for your journey. We have been given authority, yes, but we need to be careful to use it responsibly. Now that you know you are not on earth just to occupy space, that your existence is necessary and important, that you are not junk - help others to see the jewel in themselves too, just as your Creator sees in you. It is said that "Eyes that look are common but eyes that see are rare". People will always look but not all of them will see. When God looks at you, He sees things that everybody else ignores. Begin to understand and appreciate that you are not an afterthought or a mistake; you are just sometimes unseen by the world.

CHAPTER 5

Endurance - You Have What It Takes

THERE IS GREATNESS ON THE INSIDE OF YOU

~ DR MYLES MUNROE

"There is greatness on the inside of you". The first time I heard these words spoken to me I actually did not want to believe they were directed at me, let alone believe them to be true. I remember looking to my left and my right, trying to convince myself that those words were obviously directed at someone else sitting next to me and definitely not me. But there was no one close to me at the time, and the person was literally pointing at me as he uttered them. The scary thing for me at the time was that he said them with such determination and conviction that I was convinced that he really believed what he was saying. It felt like he believed enough for both of us. Then I started wondering how? How did he know this? He had not known me that long, so how did he know?

It's sad how most of us are more inclined to believe the worst rather than the best. Could it be that we are trying to protect ourselves from disappointment? Do you constantly think that if you don't expect much from life and yourself, then there's very little to be disappointed about just in case you do not perform to expectations or when life just doesn't turn out the way you think? Does this scenario apply to you? Are you afraid to expect a lot from yourself, because you don't believe you have what it takes? Have you tried, for example, to start a business, studying, health and fitness or even playing a sport but failed dismally the first time around and decided to give up; have you then taken this failure to be a prediction of the future endeavours in your life - meaning that you have basically written yourself off? If that is you, then you couldn't be further from the truth! I do understand where you are coming from though.

It is said that a person is the sum total of all the decisions and experiences in his/her life. The truth is that none of us is born cynical or despondent. It is our experiences and how we choose to react to them that determines our outlook on life. You will either be an optimist or a pessimist and what determines that is knowing and believing that you have the **potential** (inherent ability) and the **endurance** (what it takes) already inside of you to successfully achieve whatever you set your mind to. You were born with it! Your success is not in the hands of your parents, friends, enemies, boss, colleagues, pastor, teachers, spouse, bank or even your children. In other words, your success is not out there somewhere, hidden in some secret place waiting for you to find it if you are smart enough. No! It is in you and part of you. All you have to do is to release it. If you are not completely convinced of this, you will continue to live in self-doubt and be at the mercy of other people's opinion and (dis)approval of you for the rest of your life.

Indeed, there is greatness inside of us but how do I know this?

We were created for **dominion.** This dominion, however, is not to be over other human beings (or each other) but only over the earth and everything in it. So, in essence, before we came to earth, we were pre-loaded with everything we needed to control and manage the affairs of earth, including all (not some) of the situations we face and those we will face in future. We have the inherent ability to influence our circumstances, be they good or bad; and not to be influenced by them. That is who we are.

As we endeavour to lead and influence, life often presents us with overwhelming tasks to perform or problems to solve. As we become overwhelmed, we may tend to forget about the potential in us and become victims. Here are some key principles to tackling your journey:

1. Breakthrough the initial challenges and obstacles.

As soon as you decide to do something, it seems as though every obstacle grows ears, hears your decisions and decides to show up. Suddenly every possible opposition and hindrance in the world knows your address and pays you a visit. Ever notice how you never run out of reasons not to start when you are about to start doing something worthwhile? Sometimes genuine reasons too!

This is very strange, because in your heart you know, believe and are convicted in following this dream/assignment that you must pursue, yet starting feels like such a formidable and daunting task. This stage has a lot to do with your mind. You don't only make a breakthrough physically but mentally as well. In fact, your breakthrough begins in your mind and it works the other way too; failure also begins in your mind. It all depends on what you decide on – to fail or to succeed. The mind is a very powerful tool because it compels the rest of your body to comply with what it has decided and your life follows suit.

I have personally seen this in my own life. I recently started running long distance and had to break through all of my past prejudices. For years I had an attitude towards it; I had convinced myself that it was very hard and I could never do it. Even though growing up both in primary and high school I was an athlete, I never ran long distance. I ran 100- and 200-metres sprint and relay, did high jump, long jump and even played soccer, but I never ran 400 metres for example or anything more than that. The reason was not that I was not capable, it was because I had 'mentally disabled' myself and rendered myself incapable without even trying. In life, we attract what we believe and because I believed that, every time I attempted to run I immediately experienced shortness of breath, chest pains and would get this overwhelming feeling that I am about to faint and die. Can you imagine? So I stopped because in my mind this was just a confirmation of what I already told myself. Now that is sad and unfortunate.

"When you believe in your dream and your vision, then it begins to attract its own resources. No one was born to be a failure." Dr Myles Munroe

So, you need to make the decision to push through all the self-doubt, laziness and fear of the unknown; and once you do, it will become a little easier. This will also help you with the other challenges that will follow after you start – even though they will exist they will be less difficult than the initial ones.

2. Master the road of your journey.

Take it easy at first. Understand that this is a process and that you will have to sit before you crawl, crawl before you walk; walk before you run and run before you sprint. When you start, do not try to be at the same level as someone who has been at it for much longer than you. If you do that you are setting yourself up for failure. Give yourself a break – allow yourself to start slow and small but work systematically and with dogged intent towards your goal. By starting off like that, you give yourself a chance to learn all the contours of your journey, the bends, inclines, declines, flat surfaces, rough and smooth places, hills and mountains. This will help you to plan your journey based on the relevant information, thus helping you mitigate pitfalls and those unforeseen circumstances. When I started running I did not do this. I pressured myself into running like others who had been running long before me. I took on a long distance for beginners and I was not using the right running shoes. One morning, about a month after I started running, I felt a terrible sharp pain in both my ankles but worse in my right ankle; and both ankles were quite swollen. At first, I tried to treat myself with muscle sprays and ankle braces, thinking it was just a sprain but to no avail. Eventually, I went to the hospital and x-rays showed that I had fractured my right fibula at the ankle. So I was chair-ridden and on crutches for four months. There is always a process to be followed before any success can be achieved and it always starts at the beginning. You must be willing to follow that process to the letter for you to succeed. There are no shortcuts!

3. Refuse to be discouraged by what you hear, feel and see.

Stop believing the negative things that others say about you. How often do we 'abort' our dreams and assignments after one word from someone else? When we do this we are literally taking our life and putting it in the hands of that person and unwittingly absolve ourselves of all responsibility for our own lives. How is that, you may ask? Well…truth is life is a responsibility! All of us are responsible and should take responsibility for our own lives; and this means we cannot afford to carelessly hand it over to someone else while we sit back, relax and watch them live it on our behalf. No individual can successfully live someone else's life. The life that you've been given demands that you and only you live it; and live it responsibly, with character and integrity to the best of your ability. It is that valuable and precious – YOU are that valuable and precious. This quote by Dr Myles Munroe adequately captures this point: "Do not accept the opinions of others because they do not see what great and valuable potential is inside you".

It is important to note that negativity can come from anywhere, including people you love and trust, like family and friends. It will not always come from where you expect it to come from. That negativity, unintentional as it is, may even come from a good place or a good heart. Even good people can be bad for you. For example, people who I am quite close to often ask me, "but you are not obese, you watch what you eat and you're healthy – so why exercise?" Even though they may mean well, this could derail me from my goal. Since I am the only one who knows why I exercise and what result I want from it, I cannot expect other people to know what's in my head (my vision), can I? People commonly assume, in this case, that you are exercising because you want to lose weight but there are other reasons why people exercise, which include staying fit and healthy, to correct a medical condition or even to achieve a personal goal that they've set for themselves. The point is that you see a certain picture of yourself in your mind, a picture of what you want to achieve, which other people cannot see and you are the only one who knows who you are, what you want and where you are going.

It continues to baffle me how human beings are mostly prone to believing the worst about themselves and others, more than the positive. I recently made the decision to register and study six or seven years after I graduated. Upon submission of my first assignment, I received a very positive and encouraging review from my lecturer; I had passed with distinction. It was very difficult for me to believe the things she said about my work. At first, as I read through her feedback I thought she was talking about someone else; then later I said to myself, "I'm sure they say this to all the students, they must be generous mark-givers. It just couldn't be me. I'm sure there are many students in the class who have performed better than I have". The second assignment fetched an even better mark and they were marked by different people. After reading the second review I realised that there were similarities to the first one. Could it be true, what they are saying about me? Could I really be 'that person' they are referring to? I eventually laughed at myself after realising that these two people were not trying to do me any favours since they did not even know me. I had never met any of them. The only way they could know me enough to come to the conclusions they came to was through my work and my work reflects who I am and the potential I have. So, in reality, it is me that they are referring to. That is who I really am and all they did was confirm that which was already there in me.

So, what if I got a less positive review, would it diminish who I am? Absolutely not! We must understand that who we are is set, it cannot be changed, improved upon or made worse by any person, words or circumstance. You are already that which your Manufacturer created you to be and all you need to do is to discover who you are and constantly work towards becoming 'you'. Simply put, a less positive review would only mean having to work harder to release the latent potential that is already in me.

> "How can you believe, who receive honour from one another, and do not seek the honour that comes from the only God?" John 5:44

People speak, they have been speaking since the dawn of time and they are not about to stop anytime soon. The words they speak are both positive and negative. You cannot allow yourself to be defined by them. The best you can do for yourself is to know who you are and trust that your most authentic validation can never come from another human being; it can only come from the One who created you because He is the only one who knows the potential He has put inside of you.

4. Set your eyes on the goal.

"If you really want to do something you'll find a way; if not, you'll find an excuse" - Jim Rohn.

You must have a plan as to how you will achieve your goal. Put reasonable time frames for each step. Keep reminding yourself why you started in the first place. This will help you stay focused. Even though you may not physically see your goals fulfilled for a while, it does not mean they are unattainable. 2 Corinthians 4:18 says "So we don't look at the troubles we can see now; rather, we fix our gaze on things that cannot be seen. For the things we see now will soon be gone but the things we cannot see will last forever" (NLT). This scripture is simply talking about hope. Once hope is lost, then life itself is lost. We are nothing without hope, for it is when hope is lost that we do the most harm to ourselves and others, like taking our own lives and maliciously harming those around us. Although goals cannot be seen, they represent hope for the future (usually a better future) that one may desire. It is this hope that we tightly hold on to in the worst of times, that sees us through to the other side of our challenges. Without it, giving up is inevitable.

Having said that, it is of equal importance to ensure that, as you stay focused on your goal, you still take time to enjoy the intricacies of your journey, learn from them and reach your goal a better and improved individual.

5. Remember that endurance is more important than speed.

Although speed has its importance, endurance is better in the sense that it can keep you going even when you cannot keep speed anymore. That inner strength will keep you alive and carry you through the seasons of failure and discouragement. Your conviction to your vision or dream is inner strength and the vision-Giver is the source of that inner strength. Your Manufacturer gave it to you not only to ensure your success but also to secure His reputation. In as much as every product comes jam-packed with all the necessary tools and potential to ensure its success in its intended purpose; so do we. The manufacturer has to ensure that the product achieves its purpose. Why? To secure his reputation and goodwill. You could argue that the manufacturer does this to make money and that is true but even that comes as a result of his product's stellar reputation to fulfil its mandate or assignment. So it is with us. God, our Creator, is concerned with our success in the assignment He has given us. That is why He provides us with all the tools we will need to accomplish our purpose. In his book, *The Purpose & Power of Love & Marriage*, Dr Myles Munroe says, "God never demands anything that He does not provide for. Whatever God commands us to do, He equips us to do." Your success is guaranteed in anything that you set out to do that is in line with His assignment for you. His reputation depends on it. So, there is no need for you to be afraid to step out and do what you know you need to do. You can step out in confidence and boldness, knowing that even if you do experience failure on your way, it is only temporary; and what is inevitable in your life is a success in your assignment.

6. Expose yourself to good judgement.

"Without counsel plans go awry but in the multitude of counsellors they are established". - Proverbs 15:22

At the right time, tell someone your vision or dream; preferably people who have a role in seeing it come to pass. It is not advisable to tell every person you meet, at least not at the beginning. This is because not everyone will encourage and support you. Some people, from lack of understanding your plight, might be so negative that you are discouraged and so fearful that you decide not to even begin. Whereas once it's out there, the pressure will be on you to work on it and see it through because 'now people know' you said you would do it. So allow those good-intentioned people to hold you accountable. Listen to and consider their judgement and advice but always revert back to your vision blueprint as given by your vision-Giver.

7. Never stop learning.

May the day never come when you think you know everything there is to know with respect to your dream and stop pursuing knowledge. That would be the beginning of your end. We are encouraged to seek knowledge at every opportunity.

> "Wisdom is the principal thing; therefore get wisdom. And in all your getting, get understanding" Proverbs 4:7

8. Mentor – help others through their journeys.

Although God gives a specific vision to one person only, realising that vision takes a whole lot more people (vision enablers). Any authentic vision worth pursuing must seem overwhelming and unattainable. It must always be bigger than the vision bearer. This helps to keep you in check, knowing that you need God and other people to fulfil it. We were never meant to succeed alone. Success is meant to be attained and enjoyed by all. We all need each other to succeed. This is why we cannot achieve true success until we mentor someone. Most of us are where we are today because someone took their time to take us under their wing and mentor us. Just having someone say, "I believe in you", "You will make it", "You are doing well", "Your best is yet to come" or "There is greatness inside of you", goes a long way to giving and/ or restoring hope to someone.

9. Your success is as sure as you are alive.

How do I know this? You were built for it. No creator or inventor creates a product for failure. They all want and actually need their products to succeed. So, they make sure they equip their inventions with everything they will need to be a great success. As long as you are still alive, there's always hope. It does not matter what you've been through, how many times you have failed or what you are yet to face, that inherent ability to succeed that is already in you remains intact. All you need to do is tap into it and unlock its treasures.

CHAPTER 6

Born To Be Distinct

For me, there is one simple but practical and constant reminder of my uniqueness – my fingerprints. No human being has the same fingerprints as the next person, not even identical twins. Interestingly, another species that shares this unique quality is the zebra. According to National Geographic, no animal has a more distinctive coat than the zebra. Each animal's stripes are as unique as fingerprints - no two are exactly alike -although each of the three species has its own general pattern.

Think about that the next time you wonder why you are not like this person or when others tell you to be more like that person. We often fall into the trap of comparing ourselves to others, which usually ends with us falling short somehow; this then deepens our insecurities and perceived inadequacies. Time and again, parents rate their children's potential by comparing them to other children, be it in academics or sports or even temperament. This comparison is common amongst siblings. Have you ever been asked, "Why can't you be more like your sister? She's ambitious and outgoing" or heard the comment, "If only he could be just like his elder brother, he would be a success" or even, "Go to school and study what so-and-so studied so you can achieve greatness like they have"; "I wish you could sing like this person"; "Try to be more like this person or that group and you will make it" or a spouse could say, "Why can't you be more like so-and-so's husband/wife?" and the list goes on.

Hopefully, this will speak to every parent reading this book as I know it speaks to me. If we want to raise content and confident leaders, we need to change the way we talk to our children. From as early as possible, they need to know that who they are is enough for why they are. They don't have to try to be like somebody else because they already are somebody. Besides, trying to be like someone has no real benefit when you think about it. Let's first define the word 'like' in this context. It is a preposition meaning having the same characteristics or qualities as; similar to. It seems to me that a lot of effort is required in trying to be like other people in this context. Imagine trying to be like three, five or even more different people. How on earth would you cope? I think fatigue would be your constant companion. Is it not more beneficial to persistently pursue being your own self and becoming who you were created to be? Keep in mind that those individuals that you are told to be like, are also pursuing who they are and fulfilling their assignments; so likewise, give yourself a chance to discover and pursue yours. You owe it to yourself. You cannot be like other people. Why? Simply because you are not them; you are you! You just need to do what you need to do to succeed, that's all. Remember that it is possible to learn from others without becoming them.

Some might say they want you to be more like someone in a specific way or for you to mimic a desirable trait in a person; and as noble and understandable as that may sound, it must still be checked against the yardstick of the blueprint as designed by your Creator. Do those traits that you mimic fit into the why of your creation? If not, then by pursuing those traits, you are working hard at not being who you are. I once heard of a young man who came from generations of doctors and was himself expected to study in the same field by his father. He enrolled at a prestigious university to study medicine. After about six years or so at his graduation, the young man is said to have handed his father the certificate he was awarded. His fathers' countenance changed from proud parent to bewilderment. Then the young man began to explain his strange action saying, "Dad, I am giving you this qualification because it is yours, not mine. You are the one who wanted me to pursue it and you had your reasons why. I have never wanted to study medicine but you would not know that because you never asked me what I wanted. You wanted what you wanted and that was that. So today I'm giving you what you want and I am now going to pursue what I want, what I believe is who I am, my purpose – and that is to become a teacher".

While it is advisable and even praiseworthy not to make negative words your reality, it is also only fair to acknowledge that it is easier said than done. Owing to the different backgrounds, past experiences, education, religion and cultures (which then form our mindset and therefore our outlook on life), people generally have the strange propensity of not easily forgetting spoken words, especially the not-so-kind ones. This is very strange but true. You can have two different people tell you one positive and one negative about you, even just five minutes apart and you would be most likely to believe the negative comment. Even with just one person commenting both negatively and positively – the most likely comment you would believe is the less flattering one. The negative almost always trumps the positive. At least, that has been my experience.

However, this is not to say that all seemingly negative comments are bad and must be ignored, especially if they are of a constructive nature. There is a difference between a person who comments to 'build' you up and bring out your potential and the one who comments with the intention to crush you. Remember that even positive comments can be ill-intentioned. Which brings me to this point – it is of utmost importance that while you listen to and consider other people's comments and opinions about you, that you always revert to the blueprint of your life as designed by your Creator. Your survival depends on this! Who and what He says you are and are not, is what is true and will stand, because He is the one that fashioned you. **No one can know a product better than its manufacturer.**

Unfortunately, when we take these words to heart and believe them, we create a 'prison' or trap for ourselves that few have the fortuity of escaping. Sadly, we not only imprison our minds but also and more importantly, our potential. The word potential can be defined as having or showing the capacity to develop into something in the future or the latent qualities or abilities that may be developed and lead to future success or usefulness. So basically, potential speaks of possibilities, that is, what could be. It goes beyond what is and looks for what could be. That is why you cannot afford to 'lock yourself' in the past or even the present, whether by your own volition or by other people's opinion of you because tomorrow could very well be different. Just like the gadgets we have come to rely on so much, you and I came into this earth fully loaded with potential from our Manufacturer – potential to fulfil our assignment. That is what distinguishes you from the next person.

Having said that, let me also say that I for one really love and appreciate the fact that different does not mean better. Often we get caught in the fallacy that our uniqueness makes us better, in one way or another, than other people. The truth of the matter is that we are all equally important because what we carry inside, although unique to the individual, is of value to everyone who needs it. You exist because someone somewhere needs your gifts and talents (your potential) to survive. That is how important and necessary you are. Once you know your assignment and the potential you carry to fulfil it, you will experience certain convictions that are in line with that. Imagine for a moment if Nelson Mandela did not heed to the call of his assignment when he did? The injustice that he and others were fighting against would probably have been worse and maybe even more drawn out than it was. Yes, you could argue that if not him, then someone else could have done it, but when and how? We really cannot know that for certain, can we? I don't know many people at that moment that would do what he did the way he did it. Conviction will make you do things you could have never imagined doing. If Henry Ford hadn't kept going in the early days despite ridicule; if he had given up, chances are we would never have seen the Ford car. It's been much the same with almost every great person you could name. Viktor Frankl says, "What is to give light must endure burning," I tell you; your conviction will do that to you.

So, what do you think would happen if you do not serve your gifts to the world? Could you really stand by and watch people die of thirst, knowing very well that you have an abundant supply of water at your disposal? Remember that those gifts and talents were not given to you to keep for yourself; they are to serve mankind, thus serving the One who gave them to you in the first place. Your Creator shared them with you; surely you can also share them with others. In his book, *Maximizing Your Potential*, Dr Myles Munroe says, 'Potential is fulfilled when it is released. Potential is fulfilled when it is given to others. You cannot enjoy or fulfil your potential if you keep it to yourself'.

Have you ever heard a person say, "If it was not for this or that person helping me, I would not be where I am today" or "I would not have survived that had it not been for that person?". I have heard this more times than I can count and I have said these same words from time to time; I still say them even today. There are people who come into my life at critical moments, even without me realising that I need them at the time, but the difference they make is invaluable. These are people who have left a legacy in my life. Some stay for a long time and some don't, but they fulfil their purpose of being in my life for that period of time and that is what is important. Sometimes we get hurt and maybe even offended when people 'leave' our space but we should not be. As long as you understand this concept, you will appreciate that everyone is equipped to come into a certain situation to make a difference and provide solutions for the betterment of the recipients and then move on to the next assignment. People leaving your space is not always a bad thing – it is so that they make way for the next unique difference-makers and solution-providers. You need to look at it this way; they are not running from you but rather moving towards leaving a legacy in someone else's life. How great is that? At the same time, there are others moving towards leaving a legacy in your life. This means that you also have to be moving and striving towards leaving a legacy in others. We were all assigned to do this and be this in each other's lives; in our different ways and with our different gifts, yes but this is our task. **That is why even though we are all different, we are still equally important.** The difference or distinction, in this case, comes from the fact that each one of us is created and fashioned according to our assignment. So never second-guess how you look or your character traits for example, because **you are the way you are because of why you are,** as long as all this is within the boundaries of the Manufacturer. That is why you cannot despise or look down on other people because you understand that they are just as unique, special and called as you are. It does not matter how they look, their status, education or whether they are people of means. Every human being, across all races, even the ones which are considered poor, have dreams and aspirations. All we desire is to attain those dreams. Based on this truth, there will never come a day when it is okay to think other people are better than others.

Our uniqueness then becomes something to be celebrated and appreciated, because it gives us our value. The word value means the importance, worth or usefulness of something. We often value things and people based on their inherent ability to fulfil their purpose, e.g. street lights, television, people, etc. Consider the street light. It is not something you would give a second look at during the day when there's light. It is basically just a pole on the side of the road, until nightfall and you have to find your way home in the dark. That is when you begin to value it, because of the much needed light it will give you. Right there in the dark of night, that street light is unique, because it gives you something that 1). you need desperately at the time and 2). you cannot get from anywhere else, again at that time. The moon does the same too, in the absence of electricity. If not for the pictures and sound it projects, a television would be no different from an ordinary box resting on or hanging from a surface. The same goes for people; there are certain people that you go to for different needs in your life. For example, when you are sick you go to the doctor, not your cousin or friend. Why? His skills can solve your problem. If you have a burst pipe you call a plumber and if you are a child who is feeling hungry, you normally call Mom. While we cannot all be the same thing to everyone in every situation, what we need to understand is this - that which we are to each other when it matters the most is what makes us valuable and special. My take is that if we were all the same, life would be boring anyway. So never shy away from pursuing your assignment, because that is what sets you apart from other people. It is what makes you who you are. It is where you will find your value. Suffice to say, there is nothing you can do or say that can ever determine, lessen or add to your value. Your experiences do not and cannot cancel out your value because your value was established while you were still just an idea in your Creator's mind.

I think it is imperative to keep in mind that our gifts need to be developed and honed. Your gift is your responsibility and the quality at which you use it to serve humanity will be determined by how much you have polished it. So your uniqueness is not only in having a special gift but also in how you deliver it. Many people can sing but it is the quality of your singing that sets you apart.

We can also look at fruit trees, take the mango tree for instance, that continuously challenges me. Growing up, our most common holiday destination was my grandparent's farm. My grandad basically had everything you would find on a farm, from animals to vegetation. We specifically loved being there around Christmas time because of all the mango trees and the different types of them. We would spend the day moving from tree to tree or on a lazy day, just stay on the ground and pick the drooping ones. What challenges me is that mango trees have a lot in common, that is, they are trees and their purpose or assignment is to produce mangoes. So where or in what is their uniqueness then? You could say it is in the different types of mangoes that they produce. Yes, that is true, but then what about the ones that produce the same type of mangoes? Does this mean that there is no uniqueness there; I believe not. They may all be trees, producing the same type of fruit (mangoes), during a specific season, but their distinction lies in the quality of fruit they produce. These trees are not worried about what the other tree next to them is doing; they are only concerned about producing the best mangoes ever. That is what distinguishes them from the next tree and what do they do after they produce their fruit? They remain in their place and wait for the fruit to be picked. I have never heard of a tree advertising its own fruit and asking you to pick it over those of other trees. Instead, it is you and I that go to the tree to pick its fruit. What attracts us to a particular tree is the quality of its fruit.

Similarly, we may also find ourselves in situations which leave us wondering about our value and uniqueness; making it easy to just blend in with the environment like a chameleon and not stand out like we were created to. There is no limit to things that could potentially make us doubt our uniqueness. For example, in our careers, you find that there are managers of various departments, accountants, engineers, etc. and if you are one or more than one, you may be asking yourself, "What is it that I have to offer that will be different from what they are doing? Is it even worth putting effort into? We are all doing the same thing anyway; my work will not be different from theirs, so I'll do just enough to get by". Just like the trees, take advantage of your special ability to produce work that only you can, even in the same field as others. You have that ability within you. In music, someone might say, "What's the point of honing my skill and trying harder, I will never sing like this person or be as good as they are". Of course you will not sing like them and that's okay because you are not them. You have your own unique way of singing that is distinctive to you and therefore rare and unrepeatable. That is your signature! Humanity is waiting for it, so please be careful not to deprive the world of that rare uniqueness.

Now that we have this knowledge, we will hopefully come to discover, appreciate and celebrate our uniqueness and not try to be like other people or seek validation from creation but from our Source. I have come to realise that the glory of the inventor lies in the uniqueness of his product. So our uniqueness glorifies our Creator – He delights in the diversity of His creation. We can also put it this way, the architect or inventor cannot be experienced fully until the product manifests its identity.

We are a breath-taking reflection of our Creator!

These words by Viktor Frankl attest to how important you and I are:

"Everyone has his own specific vocation or mission in life; everyone must carry out a concrete assignment that demands fulfilment. Therein he cannot be replaced, nor can his life be repeated, thus, everyone's task is unique as his specific opportunity to implement it".

CHAPTER 7

You Are What You Think In Your Heart

THE PICTURE THAT WE HAVE OF OURSELVES, OUR SELF-CONCEPT, WILL ALWAYS DETERMINE HOW WE RESPOND TO LIFE

~ MYLES MUNROE

In general, the heart refers to the part of the human that controls the desires, emotions, hopes, dreams and other intangible parts of our being. The mind typically refers to the part of a human that controls the intellect, reason and thoughts. The Hebrew word for heart is 'lev' or 'levav' and it refers to the centre of human thought and spiritual life. We tend to think that the heart refers mainly to our emotions but in Hebrew, it also refers to one's mind and thoughts as well. So the heart denotes a person's centre for both physical and emotional/intellectual/moral activities and sometimes it is used figuratively for any inaccessible thing. Many cultures assumed that the heart was the seat of intelligence and without an advanced understanding of physiology, it makes sense. The heart is the only moving organ in the body and strong emotions cause the heartbeat to race. When the heart stops beating, a person is dead. The Hebrews were a concrete people who used physical things to express abstract concepts, therefore the heart was the metaphor of the mind and all mental and emotional activity. One more lesson we can learn from the meaning of heart is from the greatest commandment, to "love the Lord with all your heart." It means we are to use all of our thoughts as well as our emotions to love our Creator.

The biblical reference found in the book of Proverbs 23:7, "For as he thinks in his heart, so is he. 'Eat and drink!' he says to you but his heart is not with you", adds more weight to the notion of the heart not only being the centre of our emotions but also our mind and thoughts. It simply means the man referred to here is not the man his mouth speaks of or declares him to be but what his heart thinks. He is not really friendly and hospitable as his words would imply, because he offers food to his guest while begrudgingly calculating the cost. Another interesting reference in the bible is found in Proverbs 4:23, "Guard your heart above all else, for it determines the course of your life" (NLT), meaning that everything you do will be influenced by the condition of your heart.

It has been well said that **we see things not as they are but as we are.** Our thoughts and emotions can affect what we do and later on who we become. You could show one picture to five different people and ask them to tell you what they see. I can promise you that they are all likely to give you a different answer. Why? It is because every man looks through the eyes of his prejudices and his preconceived notions. Hence, it is the most difficult thing in the world to broaden a man so that he will realise the truth as other men see it. A friend or colleague could express how smart and creative your work is and depending on how you see yourself in that respect, it could be difficult for you to believe it. You could even go to the extent of justifying your disbelief by saying, "I was just lucky; it will not always be the case". For the longest time, I have heard people say 'seeing is believing' but in this context human behaviour normally subscribes to 'believing is seeing'. We believe first and then we see what we believe. Our self-concept normally originates from a number of factors, which include: birth, race, education, culture, religion, societal labels, past experiences, affluence, lack, successes, possessions, failures, rejection, etc.

Sometimes we can find ourselves in a certain environment that comes with certain influences and over time we may blend in with the said environment and start to think that we are a part of it. Once we believe that and accept it we begin to see ourselves (and others) and situations through the lens of that environment and its influences. For example, a lion does not become a sheep just because it lives amongst sheep. Neither does a person become a car just because they decide to sleep in a garage. Granted, if you stay in it long enough, your environment may begin to affect you in such a way that you start showing some of its traits and characteristics. Even then, it still does not mean you are that environment. I am reminded of a book called *Tarzan*, where a human baby is born in the jungle and when his parents get killed, Tarzan ends up being raised by the animals in the jungle. All he knows is what he has been taught by his caregivers. He communicates by making sounds and gestures like they do, he hops, runs, plays, hunts and even eats as they eat and what they eat – he seemingly becomes 'one with the jungle' and he can mistake himself and be easily mistaken by others as some of the jungle animals. No matter how much he may look, think and behave like his caregivers, he is not them. Adapting or becoming accustomed to his environment does not change the fact that he is human and as such he possesses traits and characteristics that are unique only to humans. Trapped on the inside of him is human potential lying dormant and untapped because he has not experienced living with other humans. If he were to meet another person, he would probably raise quite a number of questions. For example, assuming he has been to the river to drink, he has probably figured out what he looks like, right? So he would probably be asking himself, "Wow! Why do I look more like that creature than those around me?"; "Why can't I communicate with them?"

The best way to help Tarzan was to change his environment, that is, to change the wildlife environment to one that is more human. Admittedly, this transition was not an easy one to make due to the length of time he lived in the wild but with time it would happen because his environment had changed; therefore the lens through which he viewed himself as well as his self-concept would change. Personally, I would equate this to a life-changing episode. Imagine for a moment a room full of people from all walks of life and these people are being asked the question, "Who of you here would like to change their life for the better?" Without a doubt, every hand would be up and some may even raise both hands, all showing that every one of us wants that. Then the next question, "If you want to change your life you need to change the way you think and changing the way you think is quite an intentional and a generally demanding exercise. It is not something you do once-off but something you purposefully choose to do on a daily basis, for as long as you live. Considering this information, could those of you who still want to change their lives for the better please keep their hands raised and the others put theirs down" What do you think would happen? My guess is that not all the hands that were raised would remain in the air. Some people would actually put their hands down just because they are simply not ready to put in the work required to change their lives. Perhaps they could keep their hands up but fail to follow through and disappear when an effort is required of them. They want the end result but they are not willing to put in the effort to attain the desired result. Many of us are no different from these people. There are quite a number of things/areas we want to change for the better in our lives but we are unwilling or just too lazy to put in the effort that matches the change we want to see. We become satisfied with frivolously endowing other people with the responsibility for our own lives and continue to point fingers and blame them, absolving ourselves of all responsibility. The truth is **your life will not change for the better by mistake or magic,** no matter how much you may want or wish it to. Positive life changes just don't happen. It is only in your intentional, consistent and stubborn will to change and your effort that will help you attain that change. Simply put, it is work. Interestingly, you may have to first change the way you think about that, before you even begin to change the way you think in order to achieve the desired result.

Henry Ford said "Whether you think you can or whether you think you can't, you're right". This statement is quite profound because it tells us that our thoughts are in fact the source and reference point by which we live our lives. Our thoughts are the blueprint or foundation that influences the outcome of the building which is our life. If the blueprint and foundation are flawed, the building will have cracks. So, while a thought may not seem like a big deal, it actually is! Everyone thinks, all the time and all day. You are going to think anyway, you cannot escape it, so why don't you think thoughts that will change not only your life but also the lives of others for the better? It is unfortunate that we generally do not become what we want to become but rather what we see in the 'watering hole' of our thoughts and imagination. Let's say you were presented with two ways in which you can live your life and you had to choose one: 1. To spend your life reacting to what you do not want to be, or 2. To spend your life responsibly responding to the questions that life continues to present you with, to each moment of your calling – to your purpose? The problem with choosing the first option is that you will then have to constantly keep in mind that which you do not want to be and if there is truth in the statement that we become what we think, then you will become what you do not want to be. In this case, option two then becomes the only reasonable choice.

Usually, human behaviour follows this pattern: you think, you speak and then you act. Have you ever heard the words "think before you speak"? I have, more than once. That is because it is a general understanding that thoughts usually precede words and words usually precede action. This statement is mostly used in the context where someone has spoken words that make it difficult to believe that those words were actually carefully considered. It normally applies when a person has uttered negative or unkind words, which may leave you wondering, "did they really think about that before they spoke – because it seems unlikely that they would speak it if they did". So if our life is a direct by-product of our thoughts, is it not therefore of the utmost importance that we fiercely and jealously guard our thoughts and be vigilant about what we allow to dominate our thought-life?

Here are some keys that can help us live a life of dominion, as mandated by our Creator:

1. Change your thinking

To change your life, you must change your thinking. In order to change your thinking, you have to change what you listen to. There's a difference between what you listen to and what you hear; that is, you cannot control what you hear but you can control what you listen to. By the mere fact that people are always talking and your ears are functioning in top form, hearing is inevitable. However, listening is different because it is something you consciously choose to do. It requires concentration so that you process meaning from the words and sentences. As a result, we tend to attract what we listen to because we choose it over and over again. The meaning that we process is what we cultivate, so it follows that it will be what dominates our thought life. Take, for instance, Netflix.com, the American media-services provider. After you watch the first two or three movies, it then begins to suggest movies for you to watch going forward, based on the type of movies you watched before. We may also look at the Internet - based on the sites that you hit, more of the same type of sites will be suggested to you and continuously pop up like adverts on your screen. Whatever you cultivate will dominate. The word cultivate is a verb meaning to nurture, to promote, to encourage, to support, to develop or to improve. It's like good and evil. Good is more powerful than evil but if you cultivate evil, it will dominate – not because it is more powerful in its nature though.

So you want to change your thinking? Choose your friends carefully. This is not to say that you should go out of your way to avoid helping people! You must help anybody who is in need of help whenever you can but there is a difference between helping people and inviting them to influence you. Start hanging around people who think the way you want to think, not the way you think. Get into the habit of thinking and saying what you want to see and not only what you see all the time. What you want to see will always be less depressing than what you see – and that is simply because we are inherently hopeful beings.

2. Be teachable

Expose yourself to people who add value to your life. There is a proverb that says, 'misery loves company'. It is normally used when observing someone miserable giving others grief or just wanting to hang around people who are in the same boat. Sound familiar? For example, an unemployed person would rather be around unemployed people instead of those who are employed, I think partly so that they have a 'pity-party' where they can comfortably complain about the 30% of people who are unemployed without any opposition or interjection and go on to blame others, including the government. If they were around employed people, they would have hope because they would realise that 70% of people are actually employed and that the government is actually not as bad as they would like to believe. Whatever area you want to change or improve, you need to hang around people who have achieved in that area; instead of hating, criticizing or being jealous of them. They carry the keys to achieving your goals – they are there to show you what is possible! So, do yourself a favour and get close to them and ask them how they did it. Learn from them. The sad but necessary truth is that **your victim mentality only victimises and imprisons you and no one else.**

3. Stop making excuses

You can never change what you tolerate and what you prioritise will always be your object of pursuit. What dominates your thoughts concerning your life? Have you taken a backseat and allowed others in the driver's seat of your life? Are your thoughts dependent on what others do and say? Have you absolved yourself from taking responsibility for your life, because it's just easier that way? I remember doing that a long time ago. As I said before, my husband and I had been married for quite a while and still could not conceive a child. I was miserable and clearly only wanted to be more miserable, because I rejected every person (even family) and every opportunity that came to help me. I wanted what I wanted when I wanted it and how I wanted it. No one was going to be of much help unless they came up with a working plan for this to happen. I did not want to hear any other stories. My excuse was that no one understands my pain and my thoughts were constantly centred on not being able to conceive; so much so that I missed out on a whole lot of other precious moments that life presented because I just got stuck in one moment. I refused to be teachable. Albert Einstein said, "There are only two ways to live your life. One is as though nothing is a miracle. The other is as though everything is a miracle". Those days I lived as though nothing was a miracle except for me conceiving a child. I allowed myself to see my life through lenses of pain and my being a victim, and that eventually became how I saw myself and how I believed others see me. Due to how I chose to react to my circumstance, I was not able to see the miracles in the many different moments of my life for so many years – and that is just sad! I tolerated and prioritised my excuses and therefore could not change for the better. I got myself stuck in that rut for quite a while.

It is crucial for you to understand that any thought you may have that does not inspire hope is based on a lie. All the thoughts I had about myself back then only inspired the opposite of hope. At some point, I was full of self-loathing and suicidal because I thought this one thing automatically made me a failure and a worthless person. Yet I am not - and neither was I then - a failure and a worthless person; so those thoughts were based on a lie. I chose one moment, one sad moment to define my whole self and then I began to speak and act according to my choice. I think it is also worth mentioning that we are not powerless against our thoughts. We possess the will to change how we think. Don't we say "a wise man always changes his mind"? We do not have to be stuck in the rut of certain thoughts – we can choose because we possess free will. Viktor Frankl says, "Between stimulus and response there is a space. In that space is our power to choose our response. In our response lies our growth and our freedom". This statement is both humbling and exciting for me. It tells me that only I have control over my life. The minute I start blaming others for what happens or does not happen in my life, I have given my control to those people – this means I am 'passing the buck' of responsibility for my own life onto others. Our control is exercised in the space between what happens to us and our reaction to it. That space can determine whether you live a life of success or failure, victory or defeat or whether you are an overcomer or you are constantly overwhelmed.

A thought is a very powerful thing. It possesses the power to build or tear down, to encourage or discourage, to give life or to take life. It is a place of limitless possibilities. No one can ever tell you to stop thinking or dreaming. Such is the importance of a thought – we need to strive to always think right because everything else in our life adjusts itself to and follows our thoughts. So, guard your thoughts, because nothing will really change until you change how you think!

CHAPTER 8

Called To Live Beyond Your Limitations

WHEN YOU FEEL LIKE YOU'VE DONE ALL YOU CAN, YOU
HAVEN'T. YOU'VE ONLY DONE WHAT YOU KNOW TO DO
BUT NOT ALL YOU CAN

The best illustration I can use to give you a picture of the depth and vastness of who you are and your potential in relation to your assignment is to liken it to water. A few years ago, I had the privilege of cruising to an island in the east of Africa. From the balcony of my cabin, where I sat for hours on end on most afternoons into early the evening, I watched the sea. It was so peaceful, so serene. I took in its beauty, especially its golden glow at sunset, and the endlessness of it all. I would describe water as endless, boundless, free, agile and unbiased. It will go wherever it is sent to fulfil an assignment. It is governed by its own laws so it will not compromise itself even when there is a lot at stake. For example, if an unexperienced swimmer jumps into a body of water and finds them self drowning, the water will not then turn itself into grass just to save this person. It remains what it is - water; just as it does when an experienced swimmer jumps in. Also, water can be used in small quantities and in large volumes. You decide how much you want – all the water does is remain available. Another observation is that water can take on different shapes and sizes, depending on the container it is placed in at the time for a specific purpose. It will not say to the pourer, "Don't pour me into this container because last week I was in it and didn't like it" or "This container is too good for me, I feel like I don't measure up".

This is what water realises:

1. It knows that it is more than enough to fulfil an assignment. It understands that those containers are only temporary things; they will not and cannot last forever. So, it does not limit itself to only one or a few containers.

2. It also understands that fulfilling its purpose will require many more containers of different types, even some with chemicals to treat it for different durations - so it cannot lock itself up in the experience of one.

3. It knows that the containers are only a means to an end and not the end. Again, their transiency ensures this.

4. It does not compromise its natural form to take that of the different containers. It knows what and why it is and remains as such!

Hopefully, this analogy has given you some understanding of who you are and the importance of your full and rich potential in fulfilling your assignment on earth. Your experiences, people's opinions and their labels and even the self-imposed labels are only the containers that must contribute to you fulfilling your assignment. While they may be a necessary part of the journey, they are not the whole journey and they are certainly not the destination. They will constantly change, so you also need to be unabatingly connected to your Source so that you can always be reminded of who and why you are. That way the ocean of your experiences will not swallow you up.

Every so often we limit ourselves from living life to the fullest because of our past experiences. We hide behind our perceived failures and get stuck on those experiences, which seems to incapacitate us because we then cease to function and just 'camp' there. It is imperative to take cognisance of the fact that our limitations only create suffering. Most of us stay in our failures, successes, strengths and weaknesses until we adapt and begin to believe that those things are what define us, consequently stifling our potential. Somehow, we must come to understand and accept the fact that none of these things above make up who we are and so they do not have the power to define or limit us unless of course, we give them the power to do so. It is all up to you. Truth is there is much more to you than your experiences and people's opinion about you. These are just events that are taking place in the journey of your life. That is the long and short of it. Who you are was established long before the events came along, so they are not only a secondary factor but also a passing (transitory) one at that. So, why would you worry so much about something that is not permanent, to such an extent that your best full life is compromised? Why allow the bitterness of winter to numb your senses in such a way that you are unable to explore and enjoy the warmth of summer when it arrives? Both winter and summer are sporadically constant but also fleeting; so taking your whole future and locking it up inside the limitations box of 'winter' would be nothing short of rendering a huge injustice, first to your Creator and then to yourself. You would be compartmentalising your potential. Talk about limitations! To live your purpose-driven life to the fullest, you need to see beyond winter, because summer will definitely come. Be careful not to let summer limit you too. Live above the seasons of your life.

Having said that, I believe we also need to acknowledge that we have limitations. That is the first step towards addressing them. John Wooden is quoted as saying, "Don't let what you can't do prevent you from doing what you can do". Quite a thought-provoking notion, don't you think? **Some of the factors that contribute to our limitations are:**

- **Fear** (of the unknown, of failure, etc.). I have never heard of anyone who said they have a fear of success. This tells me that fear in this context can be attributed or linked to the negative parts of our lives. This then tells me that fear is not and should not be a normal and healthy part of our life. Written in the manual that you and I came with, is a clear instruction from our Inventor which states that we are not to live in fear, as He has not given us a spirit of fear but of boldness and soundness of mind. I am not saying that we are not to feel fear – I know there are times when I do. There is nothing wrong with feeling fear; the problem arises when we allow the feeling to take root and we start acting on it and partnering with it. This means that we are in agreement with it. We can nip fear in the bud by replacing it with what we know we have - boldness and a sound mind.

- **Age** - you may feel you are too young or too old to start or even complete your assignment. You may have even thought that you do not have the strength. People may have pointed this out to you or you could just be self-limiting. What you need to realise is that your Creator will never cease to have use for you as long as you are alive. So as long as you still have breath in you, rest assured that you have greatness that the world is waiting to experience. Previously, we talked about our value and how it is attributed to our gifting in fulfilling our assignment. The truth of the matter is people do not follow you because of your age, possessions, level of education or status, no! People are attracted to you because of your gift. That is why once you stop exercising your gifts and their fruits are no more, you may notice the people around you start to disappear. When this happens, please don't take it personally. They are not conspiring against you – it's just that it was never about you in the first place, it has always been about the gifts that your Manufacturer gave you for the purpose He assigned to you. So as long as your gifts are intact and your assignment is still unfulfilled, there is work to do and your age is least important, therefore, it cannot be an issue.

- **Peer pressure** – Peer pressure is mostly associated with young people in their teenage years, yet it affects many adults as well. Simply put, peer pressure is the influence of members of a peer group. We were recently given the responsibility of staying with my young nephew during his last year of high school. His school is approximately one and a half kilometres from our house and while the possibility of him walking seemed plausible, we also agreed that it may be a bit too much, especially if it's to and fro. During these discussions with his parents, it was suggested that he ride a bicycle to school to alleviate the pressure of walking and he said a very polite but firm, "No, thank you. I would rather walk". By this time, we were thoroughly confused as to why he would say that. He went on to explain that none of the kids at school go on bikes and so it would look very weird if he was the only one to do so. What if instead of weird, all the other students also began to use bikes, thereby making him a trendsetter? I even voiced this to him but he said, even so, he did not think he wanted to be a trendsetter in that way. Notice that his reason was not that it is illegal or even that the school policy does not allow it. It was about what the other kids would say. Talking about clothes, later on, he said that he would not wear certain types of clothing to school because of the same reason. He went on to say that if he were the only student at the school he would but since there are other students who will not be shy to point that out, he just cannot wear certain types of clothing to school – he'll gladly wear them at home but not to school. You can imagine how ridiculous I thought this was. It wasn't even about his personal choice; whether he liked them or not, it was about his peers. We arranged morning transport for him but in the afternoon he walks home – he said he would rather do that than ride a bicycle. It's just so sad and unfortunate that we could miss out on so many opportunities, just because we prioritise the opinions of others above all else. It is not fair to yourself and to your potential.

- **Resources** – This could be time, money or possessions. The first thing you must realise here is that what your Creator calls for, He will certainly provide for. We have established that no creator will set his product up for failure. It would be illogical and self-defeating to do so. Allow me to confirm this by quoting from the very manual we came with, in Isaiah 58:11: "The Lord will guide you always; he will satisfy your needs in a sun-scorched land and will strengthen your frame. You will be like a well-watered garden, like a spring whose waters never fail" (NIV). This speaks to me of provision. This word is made up of two words, pro and vision. The word pro in this context means 'for' and some synonyms for pro include 'favouring' and 'with'. Your vision is birthed from your purpose – it is your purpose in pictures. So, your Maker is saying that, even before He gave you that vision, He had already provided every resource you could need to go about it successfully and He only provides for what He calls for and not what we think we want or are comfortable with Him calling for. That is an important truth to always keep in mind. It will save you from being busy but not effective, leading to inevitable suffering. Our Maker is ready and able to put His name behind His purpose and plans for us, but He cannot back up our own plans. This would be similar to a product telling its designer, "I know you have this plan in mind, that is why you created me the way you have but I think I'll change it now. I have a better plan than yours and will start implementing it now". The designer would have to let that product be because his name and reputation depend on his 'original' plan, not the new one. So what we can conclude from this is that **the inventor cannot change himself to suit the invention. Instead, it is to the advantage of the invention to align itself with the plans of the inventor, in order to ensure that it continues to function perfectly and get the assignment done.**

• **Being a know-it-all.** There aren't many people who have achieved much success by limiting themselves only to what they know at the time. One way to ensure growth is by acquiring more knowledge. It does not matter how much you know already, there will always be something that you do not know that could open your eyes to possibilities that you never thought were feasible. By thinking that your current knowledge is sufficient for fulfilling your assignment, you are actually limiting yourself to only what you know, which is unfortunate.

In addition to acknowledging our limitations, here are some precautions we can take to mitigate our limitations:

1. Know yourself (purpose)

Make it a priority to discover why you are so you will understand better how you must function. The key to personal fulfilment is in knowing what you need to do and then proceeding to pursue that assignment. I personally believe that a product is most successful when it is doing what it was created to do, how it was created to do it and when. That is when its potential is maximised.

The discovery of purpose will also help you to identify your strengths, which is something you can focus on and also derive support from as you deal with the challenges that you will experience in the pursuit of your purpose.

2. Separate yourself from labels, past experiences and people's opinion of you

Admittedly, this is easier said than done but it is possible. Once you come to grasp the transience of such things in your life, you will come to the realisation that these things do not equate to who you are. They are just bumps, humps, stones and potholes on the road that you are travelling and they remain as such. They do not automatically become who you are just because you happened to encounter them. Besides, as you continue on the road, you will encounter different obstacles from time to time and yours is only to conquer and pass; NOT TO BECOME THEM! It is sad that even your last success can become a limitation. Dr Myles Munroe says, "The greatest enemy of progress is your last success". Getting hung up on the past, whether good or bad, is a trap because you cannot move into the future, which is where you are headed anyway. You become a prisoner of that past.

3. Stay clear of the comparison trap

Constantly comparing yourself to others will eventually keep you trapped in a rut of disappointment and discontentedness. Again, they are not you and you are not them. Your purpose and therefore your potential will not be the same. They are running in their lane pursuing their assignment and you also need to stay in yours and do the same. Instead of being covetous of their perceived success, work at achieving your own. If they are successful in their assignment, you too can be in yours. This quote by Wayne Dyer puts perspective to this thought:

> "My goal is not to be better than anyone else but to be better than I used to be"

Do not measure your success by looking at what others have done but measure it by what you have done compared to what you are supposed to do (your assignment). Your success cannot be measured by the performance and opinions of others. Your goal should always be to grow; always pushing the boundaries; always stretching yourself in every area within the boundaries of your assignment. Being satisfied with what you are now and constantly comparing yourself to other people is a sure way to keep yourself imprisoned in the limitations loop. So, keep moving because even those who are in their assignment can get run over if they stay in one place and don't move forward.

4. Gain knowledge

Growth is imperative and the one way we can ensure growth is to acquire more knowledge and actually apply it in our pursuit of purpose. This is what it means to exercise and hone your gifts. This is how I see it: our gifts and talents could be likened to a muscle and if that muscle is not physically stretched by exercising on a regular basis, it will not grow to its full potential. In fact, it may even regress and become worse than it was in its original state. What you do not know can be dangerous in the sense that it may prevent or delay the next level of achievement in fulfilling your assignment. Actually, come to think of it, we should be more concerned about what we do not know than what we know. Why? What you know you already know and it cannot do much more for you than it already has. Getting more informed will very likely increase your potential to achieve more than what you have achieved so far.

5. Believe that you are enough for your purpose

Believe that you are worthy of and enough for your assignment. No one else can do it like you, not because you do it better but because you do it as only you can and that is enough. Remember that the One who created you is not trying to make you into something - He has already done that. What He is doing now is trying to reveal the real you to yourself and to humanity. So believe your Creator's report of your potential and not the world's, because only an inventor can determine his product's potential. What I like about potential is that it focuses on possibilities and not only on what is, or your current state. This means that neither yourself nor other people can keep you in any situation because it can change.

My question then to you is: what would be possible for you if you could overcome those thoughts that limit you? The truth is nothing can stop you getting to the top except you and nothing can limit you, except you.

I recently discovered self-imposed limitations in my exercise routine, namely jogging. When I started out I would have 'rest landmarks' where I would stop running and just walk briskly for a short while and then start jogging again. As time went on, I began to look forward to those landmarks. By the time I got there, my chest would feel like it was about to explode and my body was just about to give up. Now I am not saying that this is wrong, at least not in the beginning, because it stretched me towards that particular goal at that time. The problem began when, after being at it for a while, I was still looking forward to the same rest stops when I was well and able to go much further without resting. I had the strength and willpower to do so but couldn't because I was still stuck in the past. Just after I would start jogging my mind would remind me of the rest stop and before I knew it my chest and body would be acting accordingly. Although not wrong at first, at that time, those rest landmarks became a limitation to me. They were hindering my progress. I could have easily just remained in that comfort zone, justifying my actions (or lack of, for that matter) with the fact that I was still jogging anyway, it's not like I had stopped. Instead of realising that it is not just about jogging in itself but also about growth and progress in that area… to be the best I possibly can be and I cannot achieve that by staying in a comfort zone. So what I do now is every time I jog I try to do more by running just a little further than the last time…just a little further than the last 'rest landmark'. It is in small increments but my mind and body eventually adjust to them. I know I can do more because I am wired that way. You see, potential by its nature dictates that we should not be the same tomorrow as we are today. So do not allow your limitations to hinder you in such a way that you die without using your full potential.

So, What Are You Waiting For?

FEELING GOOD ABOUT DOING THE RIGHT THING IS NOT
A PREREQUISITE FOR DOING THE RIGHT THING. DOING
THE RIGHT THING IS A RESPONSIBILITY!

G enerally, human beings do not have a good or healthy
perception of work. If you were to interview people and ask
them what their feeling towards work is, you probably would get
very few positive responses, if any. At one point, before I gained
some understanding, I was also in agreement with this perception.
There are those of us who feel that work is a curse which is the
result of the fall of man, an unfortunate reality of life that we must
trudge through, an unavoidable burden to be endured or even
an unsympathetic and inescapable slave master. Most of us feel
trapped by it but that is only because we are not operating with
our unique gifts. No product can feel trapped while becoming
what it was created to be...instead it thrives. Unfortunately, it
is this attitude that becomes an impediment to us releasing and
maximising our potential. Allow me to explain: as far as the fall

of man, the word 'work' came as an instruction before the fall. It came together with the mandate to 'dominate and subdue' the earth, which then becomes difficult to associate with a curse. We have learnt that to dominate means to manage, to rule, to govern, to control, to influence, to lead; but how you may ask? In our different areas of gifting, that is our work. Interestingly, the word 'work' in Greek is the word 'ergon', which means to become. The word 'become' implies an ongoing state or process of becoming something or someone. So work in this context is not meant to be a curse but actually a blessing because it gives us the endless opportunity to become our authentic self. To become what we ought to be at any given moment, to correctly respond to the calling of life as it comes and to remain conscious of something beyond ourselves - which is our assignment. That is our responsibility!

Look, whether you believe it or not, **you are necessary!** The story of creation always intrigues me because it actually proves this necessity. The first command from the Creator brought light into existence, but this was only after He observed that only darkness existed "in the face of the deep". So in essence, what would you say happened here? **A need necessitated the existence of light!** Note that the light did not come to cancel out the darkness or to be superior or even inferior to it. The light came so that the darkness would not be permanent, it came to establish day from night. It came in its authentic self to play the unique role that only it can play. Question: Could it be that you came so that a person or a group of people's suffering would not last forever, that because you live someone can have hope? We all know and value all the advantages that light affords us. Actually, we are mostly a little more productive during the day than at night and if we need to work at night we use 'look-alikes' like electricity and battery powered tools. Although over the years some people have made the darkness seem like a bad thing because of their actions and experiences, darkness also has its place. For example, being the very light sleeper that I am, I for one appreciate the darkness at night because the darker it is, the better I sleep. There are other advantages to darkness, like for instance the moon. Would we ever see it in broad daylight? Sometimes yes... However it shines beautifully in the dark sky and that is when it is at its best because its value becomes evident at night; not to mention the much-needed light it provides us as well. The same applies to the stars. We are able to appreciate them at night because that is when their beauty is optimised.

Likewise, there is a reason that necessitated your existence. You are **that** important, so do not let anybody or your past, current and future circumstances tell you otherwise. For some of you, this is only a reminder but there will be some who are making this discovery for the very first time. Whichever category you may fall under, knowing this truth will prove profitable. When understood and accepted, it can potentially mitigate a vast number of the curveballs that life would throw at you. Being convinced and confident of this truth will ground you like a tree that is so grounded by its roots that even when the winds blow from all directions, the rain and the seasons come and go, it remains. Like the tree, all you do is adjust yourself according to the seasons, so that you not only merely live through them but victoriously so – in other words, you will live your life in such a way that you **don't become your seasons**. You experience them and take lessons from them but you never become them. You remain the authentic tree that you are.

Knowing you are necessary also comes with the understanding of your value and your importance; and therefore, hopelessness to the point of giving up on your life will no longer be an option for you. You may be saying to yourself, "but it is not as simple as it sounds". I agree, maybe it really isn't. I am not saying that you will always feel on top of the world and that you will not feel hopeless at one point or another! Experiencing the feeling of hopelessness is one thing but being stuck in it is another. The only thing standing between you being stuck in an existential vacuum and hope is you knowing and being constantly reminded that you are necessary and therefore more important and more valuable to humanity (your children, spouse, friends, parents, colleagues, etc.) than you can ever imagine. You will also realise that you are valuable even to the people whom you are yet to meet and change their lives for the better. If you give up to the point of taking your own life for example, who do you think is going to meet that need? Those lives are likely to remain the same or sadly become worse because you failed to recognise your value and importance - because you failed to recognise and fill your place in the puzzle. Remember that there is always someone's breakthrough waiting on the other side of your obedience! There are great things which cannot be achieved, lives which will not be changed for the better, songs that will not be sung, books and poems that will not be written and inventions that will not be realised if you are not around. A ten thousand piece puzzle will not give the complete picture if it's missing one piece, no matter how 'almost complete' the picture looks – it will still be incomplete. Why? That one piece, no matter how seemingly insignificant, is necessary and therefore valuable and important for completing the picture. Do you realise that no other piece but that specific one will do – no other piece for that specific puzzle will have the same shape, texture and size as the missing one? No other piece can be the perfect fit for that missing space. It is the only one that will do. You too are the perfect fit for a missing space in life's puzzle and that is why you are here. That is how valuable and important you are and if you did not know this before, hopefully, you know it now.

Allow me to clarify with the following story: A man in his mid-forties (Tim), who was also a husband, a father and a provider lost his job and spent months after that looking for another one to no avail. Over time, Tim became very depressed and despondent. He began to question his usefulness, whether his life meant anything after all. If he could not provide for his family then where was the value in his existence? He became aloof and irate, further straining relations at home. His wife had offered to get a job and help out in the meantime but even that was not enough to encourage Tim. On the verge of giving up, Tim decided to go and speak to a friend who pointed out to him that his value was actually not in the material things he could do for his family but rather in his authenticity. His friend went on to tell Tim that while the material things are important, they are only a by-product of his value and not the actual value. He learnt that his family values him as a unique gift to them and that they probably would not exchange that for anything. They value his function as a husband and father more than his position or status. He told him that there were still things he could do, different ways in which he could still serve his family. Just taking the time to talk to his wife, being present and playing with his kids, showing an interest in their lives and being involved with what they are dealing with on a daily basis, for instance, is of more value to them than he could ever imagine. Tim's friend also helped him realise that he was not the only one in this difficult situation, his family was in it too and chances are that they too were experiencing the same feelings and emotions. They are not against him but for him. His friend then concluded by asking him this question: "As things stand now, if you were to ask your children to choose between having an unemployed dad who cannot materially provide for them or not having a dad at all, what choice do you think they would make?" Tim left with a renewed sense of value. He remained cognisant of the fact that he still had a lot to work through but he was definitely encouraged and some hope was restored.

Among the many reasons or causes for untapped potential or the fear of responding to our calling, there is one that I would like to discuss. It is neither the only one nor the worst but it has certainly been an issue in my life personally and I also know it has been and still is the same for many others as well - and that is the fear of man. The fear of man creates an unusual appetite for the approval of man. People who work hard for recognition are usually working hard for identity. The thought is that the applause of man will give them a personal identity, but it doesn't, because any identity attained through the applause of man will need to be sustained through the applause of man. We are so conscious of and constantly worrying about what other people will say or what they think about us that eventually our authenticity becomes obscured in our quest for approval and acceptance. Sadly, we cannot climb out of the limitations of our belief, until we change that belief. You simply cannot be authentic whilst living in fear of man. In order to keep man's approval, you may have to compromise a bit of yourself constantly. You will find that you constantly have to adjust yourself to man's fleeting opinions about you and you will inevitably begin to believe lies about yourself. The fear of man opens you up to insecurities, even more fear and self-doubt and eventual hopelessness when you feel you aren't measuring up to expectations. **The fear of man compromises the integrity of your authenticity!** The only trust and security a product has is not in itself, in other similar products or even in the competition – but only in its inventor. Outside of a meaningful relationship with its creator, a product can be vulnerable and therefore prone to experiencing great insecurity; but it can find genuine and unconditional security only in its inventor and the potential that its inventor deposited in it.

Here are a few repercussions of the fear of man in relation to answering your calling:

1. Because you are concerned about the opinion of other products rather than those of your inventor, you may compromise what you can do (your potential) and focus on things that you probably cannot do because you are not wired that way.

2. Just like a dislocated joint, the fear of man causes dysfunction in that it dislocates you from your necessity – your usefulness and effectiveness.

3. Fear causes you to lose sight of your potential, thereby losing your courage. You then take a 'safer' path – according to whom or what you fear.

4. The lies you begin to believe get you to shift your focus. You become a 'safety expert' in that you will be afraid to do anything until you are sure you can do it – that surety coming from others and not from your potential.

5. Lies also distort the truth. As you strive to be what man

expects, you will only be reminded of what you lack or your shortcomings, so that pursuing your calling appears to be an unattainable goal, a bigger problem than the solutions you carry in your potential. As with good and evil and love and fear, the truth is more powerful than a lie. A lie in its nature is not powerful...that is unless or until you cultivate it.

6. The fear of man may even force you to take shortcuts in some cases and shortcuts disprove potential.

One of the greatest regrets that people have when they are faced with the end of their existence here on earth is that they lived their lives according to the expectations of people around them and not according to their dreams. The fear of man will always keep you from your Creator's ultimate and best path for your life. Did you know that your necessity is neither for nor about yourself (the individual) but your necessity is primarily valuable and important as it relates to other people? Otherwise, it would be like you needed yourself, so the Creator created you - for yourself - which is both highly improbable and amusingly absurd. There is just too much 'self' in there. Of course, an individual can benefit from his/her authenticity but that is not the primary focus. The primary focus is humanity and how you can use your uniqueness to change the world for the better and leave a legacy for coming generations. Humanity should finish better - just because you lived! Your creator saw a need that only you could meet in your own unique way, so He created you and you are responsible for correctly responding to the questions life constantly asks you; ensuring your continuous necessity. Like Tim, please do not find your value in things you can do or things you have (be it now or in future), but find it in your calling. Tim's calling at that moment was to be a husband and a father. A working husband and father would obviously be a bonus but his primary calling was to be a husband and father to the best of his ability. Your value is in your authenticity. Dolly Parton says, "Find out who you are and do it on purpose". The question is, "what humanity will lack because you fail to live out your potential?" Do not overwhelm yourself by trying to do and be everything all at once, eventually burning yourself out. We now know that your life is made out of different moments, so live it from moment to moment. Even though purpose can be discovered in its entirety all at once, it is pursued and attained from moment to moment, not at the same time. It is in those different moments – whether in joy or suffering - where we find meaning for our existence.

So I want to encourage you, instead of the opposite: dare to want to be different (because you already are). Dare to challenge whoever and whatever challenges your authenticity. Dare to rise, step out of the box and recover your buried authenticity that you compromised in order to fit into what the world around you considered appropriate. Dare to refuse to make yourself small so everyone else can feel good in your presence. You must decide if you are going to be a creator of fact or a creature of circumstance? Are you going to put colour into your environment, or, like a chameleon, take the colour of your environment? I dare you to **live in the question and not the answer**. In other words, be constantly concerned more about the need that necessitated your existence and meeting it, rather than the accolades and feelings you get once you have done so. You and I are responsible for constantly transcending beyond what is, and striving towards what ought to be. Living in the question will help you to live more in the future than in the present or the past. It is easier said than done, I know, but it is possible. How you may ask? Personally, I think it's a matter of setting the centre of your thoughts to it. We have learnt that whatever we prioritise we pursue, so when you intentionally fix your thoughts on what is true, honourable, right, pure, lovely, admirable, excellent or praiseworthy; you will find living in the question surprisingly within reach. Unless you do something beyond what you have done, you will never grow, so please, do try this at home! Living in the question will keep you focused and grounded. It will give you true freedom. Contrary to the misconception, this freedom is not the ability to **do what you want but** the ability to **do what is right**. Such is our responsibility towards the constant questions that life poses to us in the different moments that make up our life. As you answer those questions, serving your gifts to humanity, don't be too concerned with big numbers but be concerned with big people, because every human being is big according to the Creator. German writer and statesman Johann Wolfgang von Goethe said, "If we take people as they are, we make them worse. If we treat them as if they were what they ought to be, we help them become what they are capable of becoming". We can also apply this principle to ourselves. Simply put, be genuinely concerned about people and love them. You cannot truly serve them if you don't and that is a fact. Unfortunately, we live in a world where the concept of genuine concern and love for people is fast becoming a myth. Keep in mind that the value of your life is in your contribution and not in its longevity; it is in your function, which is unchanging, because it is found in who you are and not in your position, which is transitory.

To add more clarity, let us explore the meaning of these two words.

According to the dictionary, the word function as a verb means to work, to perform, to operate and as a noun, it means an activity that is natural to or the purpose of a person or thing. A simplified definition of the word position is a place where someone or something is located or has been put. For example, a person who is gifted in marketing possesses the grace or fluency to function in that gift. Now, at work, he may be given or put in a position which requires his gift but the position does not determine his function and him functioning in his gift is not dependent on a particular position. The truth is, positions are determined by people and if a person puts you in a certain position, it follows that they can also remove you from the said position because they put you there in the first place. That is why position is fleeting. If this person is relieved of their job or position at work, it cannot and should not be a train-smash for them because they get to take their marketing gift with them and they can still function in that gift in any other place where that gift is necessary. It is important not to confuse the two.

Your contribution determines the legacy that you will leave behind. I once heard of a seemingly amusing but valid explanation of legacy – that is, when other people cry louder than your closest relatives at your funeral because of the meaningful contribution you made in their lives. Granted, this statement may be comical but it is just as reflective. Please be aware that there are situations you will face that may cause you to be discouraged and even despair in pursuing and fulfilling your purpose but none of them can change it or make it obsolete.

About two years ago on my morning jog, I came across a certain middle-aged woman who, as I was approaching, stopped and looked like she wanted to talk to me. It was usual to come across a lot of people walking up and down going about their business, so even though I normally do not like to 'break' or disturb my exercise routine, I decided to slow down and hear what she had to say. I thought to myself, "Maybe she is in some kind of trouble and needs my help, and besides, she's someone I sometimes come across on this route so there's low risk of stranger-danger". So I slowed down and walked towards her. The words that proceeded from her mouth proved to be something I could have never expected. She looked at me dead in the eyes and said, "You know, I've observed you jogging here for the past couple of months, and I have to wonder why you continue to do so because it is not working. You are not losing any weight. Actually from where I'm standing it looks like you are gaining more than losing it". With that, she was done talking…so this is what she felt the need to stop me from my jog to say? Awkwardness swiftly ensued, and as she stood there still looking at me, I quietly asked myself with mild disbelief, "Could she be waiting for a response…like really?" To say I was taken aback would be the understatement of the century. I stood there, thankfully speechless for a few seconds, before abruptly resuming my jog, leaving her standing there. I honestly did not know how to respond to that, so I decided not to. At that moment I did not trust myself to say anything that would not go awry, so out of respect for the both of us, I left.

I believe every honest person would agree that those words had the potential to annihilate any dream that I may have had, whether it was to lose weight, to maintain, or just to keep fit for health reasons. Her unsolicited words were harsh and discouraging. At the time I still had about two kilometres to go and even though at first I was angry and offended at such mean-spirited audacity, I did not give up, I continued to jog. I had to remind myself of the purpose or reason for running, and said "It's because I love doing it. I love living an active, healthy lifestyle, and it makes me feel good about myself". I figured that that was what life was asking of me at that moment, and if I lost any weight it would be an added bonus. The main purpose for me was not to lose weight, but even if it was, she did not know the intricacies of my journey; she would not have been privy, for example, to my diet, when I started, how many times I jog per day, my goal weight, my start weight, etc. Besides, who is to say at the time that her observation was correct? If someone else in the same situation were to be asked to comment, is there a possibility that they would differ? I believe so! You must understand that people will always have varying and often passing opinions of you; the only thing that remains unchanged is your purpose and potential. Generally, human beings have different reasons for doing the things they do, even though it may be the same thing. This is what that lady did not understand. She just assumed her own reasons for my jogging and attempted to impose them on me. She did not know me or what I am about; therefore it would have been pointless to get stuck on her reality of me and define myself by it. I knew 'why' I was exercising, and so I realised that I could bear almost any 'how', even in the face of possible discouragement.

Do not give up - People have been saying things, doing things and changing their minds about those things for time immemorial; they are not about to stop anytime soon. The world will try to impose its standards and labels on you, daring you and sometimes even compelling you to see life through its lenses; but do not allow that to tamper with your potential. Take only what is in line with your assignment, and leave the rest for those who think it's the right thing for them. A person who does not give up is difficult to defeat. If you feel hopeless because you cannot change a situation, then challenge yourself to change. Do not define yourself by what has happened or by what you think may happen. Ralph Waldo Emerson says, "What lies behind us and what lies before us is small matter compared to what lies within us". You are your Creator's unique invention and who He says you are is much bigger than what has been done to you or what you have done/where you have been or even what you possess. Your authenticity is actually what gives you not only the courage but more importantly the right to responsibly face the future with success, no matter what it may come with. You were born with the gift of authenticity; do not allow yourself to finish off as a copy of someone else. Stay true to your purpose.

APPENDICES

Appendix A

Self-Appraisal

Who am I? (Describe yourself as you see yourself realistically)

_____

_____

What does my family want me to be? (You may write a separate answer for each family member)

_____

_____

What do I want to be and why?

_____

_____

What are my potentials?

_____

_____

What are my obstacles?

_____

_____

What can I do to realise my potentials?

_____

_____

What would the first step be?

_____

_____

What can I do to overcome my obstacles?

_____

_____

What would the first step be?

_____

_____

Appendix B

Value Questionnaire

What does the word 'value' mean to you?

_____

_____

What makes a thing or object valuable?

_____

_____

What makes a person valuable?

_____

_____

Do you think all people are valuable, and why?

_____

_____

Do you think value is general, uniform, or unique to the individual? Why do you think so?

_____

_____

How do you relate with the things and people that you value in your life?

_____

_____

Please state True or False on the following statement: We (humans) normally treat others according to how much we value them

_____

_____

Do you think that value is always seen or recognised?

_____

_____

Is there a difference between *ignorance of value* and *absence of value?*

_____

_____

Do you think that the ignorance of value automatically translates to or means the absence of value?

_____

_____

In your life so far, have you ever found yourself in a situation where you actually believed that the ignorance of value means the absence of value?

_____

_____

In your opinion, how is a person's value determined? Is it inherent (inborn/permanent/built-in/inseparable) to him/her, or does it come from other people's opinions and/or things?

_____

_____

Would you agree that the value of a product is determined by its manufacturer, and not by the consumers or other products?

_____

_____

Please state True or False on the following statement: Unseen or unrecognised value is still value

_____

_____

Do you recognise your own value? If not, why do you think this is so?

_____

_____

What can you do to recognise your value?

_____

_____

Would you help others recognise their own value if you had the opportunity to do so?

_____

_____

Do you think it is important to recognise and celebrate ones' value and that of others? Why do you think so?

_____

_____

REFERENCES

Munroe, M. (2008) *Maximizing Your Potential: The Keys to Dying Empty*, Destiny Image Publishers Inc., Page 127

Munroe, M. (2002) *The Purpose and Power of Love & Marriage*, Destiny Image Publishers Inc., Page 213

Mwaikambo, A. (2016) *Partakers of the Divine Nature*, His Voice Today Publication, Pages 15-18

Frankl, V. E. (2008) *Man's Search For Meaning*, Rider, an imprint of Ebury Publishing, Pages 8, 12, 85. Available at: https://www.goodreads.com/author/quotes/2782.Viktor_E_Frankl?page=1,2 (Accessed: 24/05/2019)

Fabry, J. (1988) *Guideposts To Meaning: Discovering What Really Matters*, New Harbinger Publications Inc., Pages 153-154

Tverberg, L. A. (2003) *Levav - Heart, Mind.* Available at: http://www.egrc.net/articles/Rock/HebrewWords/levav.html (Accessed: 23/05/2019)

SPECIAL
TRIBUTE

A Special Tribute to the Life and Legacy of Drs Myles and Ruth Munroe 1954 - 2014

16th November 2014

MAMA & PAPA

It's been seven days now since Chief Kingdom Ambassadors; my Papa & Mama, (Drs. Myles & Ruth Munroe) were recalled back to the Home Country (The Kingdom of Heaven) in a plane crash on the 9th of November, 2014.

It is still a very unbelievable nightmare for me. Just nine days earlier on the 31st of October 2014, Dr Zondi, my husband Eric and I, saw them off at the OR Tambo Airport in Johannesburg, South Africa to go back to The Bahamas to complete preparations for the Global Leadership Summit Dr Myles hosts annually. We were actually taken aback by the fact that on this particular day, the airport personnel allowed us to take them past the check-in point and way back towards security (which is only reserved for travelling passengers – and we were not travelling at the time). As we began to say our goodbyes, which Papa ALWAYS complained about – he always said, "Oh no, it's that time again...I hate goodbyes" - it was time to let them go through security and into the waiting area to board their flight. We were sad that we had to part but were in high spirits because we were going to see them soon and we had also spent most of the month of October with them as they travelled throughout South Africa and the African continent as a whole. Little did we know at that moment that it would be the last time we ever saw them alive, spoke to them, touched and hugged them, got advice from them, got reprimanded by them, got gifts for them, learnt from them and just basically had parents.

The one thing I had come to realise about my parents is that it was almost impossible for any individual to cross paths with them; be it sharing a drink or maybe a quick greeting and handshake or taking a photo (which happened all the time – and they did it willingly and with a smile without complaining, no matter how fatigued they were from previous engagements) or even just a short word from Papa; and leave unchanged for the better, no matter how bad your situation seemed. With his big, loving, infectious, signature smile, the last words Papa said to us were, "Bye now, see ya'll next week at the Leadership Conference in the Bahamas. I love you guys a lot". He then called to Mama Ruth to hurry on with the unending hugs and with the final wave of his hand; he turned his back to us and handed over his hand luggage to the security personnel.

Let me take you back to a few hours earlier. Early that morning Eric and I were at our daughter's school attending her concert and graduation. As the event wore on, we became a bit nervous about the time because they had come in very early form Gabon and, according to Charlie Masala, their flight to Atlanta then to

Nassau, Bahamas was at 17:30 pm. So, we were supposed to be at the airport to receive them at 14:00 pm. Charlie had informed us that they had checked-in for the day at a hotel near the airport so they could rest before the long flight home. We arrived a bit early so we had lunch at the airport and decided we'd go and wait for them at the lobby of the hotel they had checked into while they were resting. We hadn't sat for a minute when we discovered that Dr Zondi was also there waiting for them. Hardly five minutes later, Papa came marching out of the elevator dragging his hand luggage and when he saw us at the lobby his face suddenly lit up and he beamed and said, "Ya'll are here already? Why didn't you wake us up, man? We don't wanna be late for our flight". At that moment Mama Ruth came behind Papa smiling warmly, holding her bag looking gracefully calm and relaxed from their rest. After some quick hugs and kisses, they briefed us on their last journey, citing how wonderful and productive it was except for the fact that they missed us. Papa actually said, "It was great and we had fun but it was not the same without you there."

It was time to move quickly across to the airport to check them in. When we got to the check-in desk, we discovered that Charlie had made a mistake about the flight times. They were scheduled to depart at 20:30 instead of 17:30. We were excited and felt so privileged to have a few extra hours with them. Although we had an appointment afterwards, we were just happy to be with Papa and Mama just for a while longer. I don't think we ever did get tired of hearing Papa talk to us about any and every subject. It was always a chance for us to learn. Little did we know that would be the last time we would see and talk to them on earth. I think the saddest thing for me now is that in August 2014 during the first-ever marriage seminar in South Africa, Mama Ruth and I had just started talking a lot and connecting at a much deeper level, besides our usual 'must-have' shopping escapades with Xoli (or Zoli, as they affectionately called her) Masala and Charisa... which I must say we absolutely enjoyed ☺. Anyway, I talked to her and got advice and a ton of wisdom concerning some areas of my life, especially my marriage. At first, when I asked her to mentor me in this respect, she gave me that 'knowing' motherly look, took my hand in hers and said, "Of course I'd be happy to... besides, what have you been waiting for all this time? We should have started this a long time ago", she said with a warm smile and an affectionate nudge on my arm. I got to spend even more time with her when they came back in October and got to learn much more from her. Now I wish I had started much earlier.

So, we checked in their bags and decided to walk to a close-by restaurant and the five of us spent the next two-and-a-half hours having drinks and chatting. Papa joked about how Charlie got the times wrong because he mixed it up with the birth of his daughter. The Masala's were expecting a baby girl who was due on the next day, the 1st of November. That's why he was not there; he had to be at the hospital. Papa then brought us up to speed with details of their last few trips (which included lots and lots of photos on his iPad) and simultaneously expressed his excitement and great expectations about the upcoming Global Leadership Conference in the Bahamas.

Sitting there with them seemed so normal. In fact, it was normal; just as normal as all the other times in the past that we had shared a meal together and talked about so many topics. Yet there was nothing normal about that particular day in the sense that it would be that very last time we would see them on earth.

Now I find myself asking this question, "If I knew then what I know now, what would I have said or done differently during those few last moments with them? Would I have asked more questions and/or hugged them more than usual, telling them how we loved and appreciated them? Would that have been enough?" Honestly, I really do not know. I have no answers to these questions. All I can do is hope and believe that they knew exactly how much we loved and appreciated them.

Papa impressed upon us the importance of immediately starting to mentor someone to take over your position as soon as you start in that position. I say impressed because he was not talking about this for the first time. He reminded us that we will not live forever and that we will not (or at least should not) stay in one position forever, so it is imperative that we train someone else to take over. He said if we stay longer than we should, we might miss out on the next step that God would want to take us to. I quote, "It is better to leave early than to stay too late. In fact, when you start in any position, plan to leave early and then leave just a little earlier than you had planned to". We actually had a good chuckle about it but he was very serious. He said it is embarrassing to stay too long until you are literally asked to leave because people don't want you there anymore.

In the meantime, quite a few people were approaching our table and asking to take pictures with them and as was the norm, they happily obliged. All the while I felt something say I should ask to sit between them and ask Eric to take a photo of the three of us and then ask Dr Zondi to take one with him. This happened about three times but I ignored it because I kept saying to myself, "Ag, it's ok. I do have photos with them and I'm still going to have much more when I see them next". Instead, Mama and I were chatting about the possibility of the Leadership Conference going back to Nassau in 2015 and the upcoming, much anticipated second chapter of the African Marriage Seminar in South Africa (also in 2015).

It's so amazing how life can change in a split-second…at the blink of an eye! At that moment as we sat there, I had so many thoughts and plans running through my head for the future (with them in it). And I know it was mutual. As we continued to discuss the state of the world and the influence (or lack) of the church in it, we were all so hopeful, so positive, so happy about what God was getting ready to do through His people and we were determined to be part of it. I am especially reminded of a young man who approached us just after we had bid goodbye to Papa and Mama and were getting ready to leave the airport. He came running to us and asked where Papa and Mama were. He explained that he had seen us sitting with them at the coffee shop and had rushed off to buy a book by Dr Myles so he could ask him to autograph it, not for himself but for his father who loved Papa very much. We apologised and told him that he was too late…that Papa had already checked-in but that he shouldn't worry because Papa would definitely be back in 2015 and he would be happy to sign his book. We gave him the Myles Munroe International Johannesburg office business card and told him to keep in touch.

Again, it's so amazing how life can throw you a curveball and force you to adjust and/or completely change your plans and life as you know it. My heart goes out to that young man. Papa talked and taught about change a lot. He told us that change is something to be embraced and not dreaded or feared because it is inevitable and it often brings new opportunities for us depending on how we view it. Even as we sat having our drinks, he did mention that change was imminent. In fact, one of the many books he has authored is titled, 'The Benefits of Change'...which I feel the need to read now more than ever. I am hoping it will help me see and understand, at least to a certain extent, God's plans and thoughts (which are always higher than ours) concerning this recent 'change', instead of trying to make sense and understand with my limited human mind.

I must admit, since their recall, especially in the first few days, I had been agonising, asking myself if they knew how much we loved them. I mean, words were spoken, love expressed from both parties, yes but did they really know how much they were loved? Did they really know what and how much they meant to us? I wondered about this until I realised that they must have known at least to a certain extent because words can be spoken but if they are not accompanied or supported by actions, they remain just that...words. In as much as they showed us love, we did too. But somehow this realisation did not 'cure' the relentless, intense, gnawing ache in my heart as I thought it would. Then about two weeks later, I had a dream. In the dream I saw Papa sitting in the front passenger seat of a car with the windows rolled down and he looked like he was having a sandwich and looking through some papers. He wore one of his signature suits (with tie and hankie) and everything was so normal it was like he was taking a short break between sessions. I walked towards the car, leaned on the drivers' door with my arm and poked my head inside through the rolled down the window of the driver's side, looked at him and said, "Papa, you do know that we love you, don't you?" To which he responded by looking up at me, gave me a brief perturbed look (like he was wondering how I could even ask him that) and then with that familiar signature smile of his, nodded and simply said, "Yes, of course, I know". After that, I immediately woke up from my sleep, sat up in bed, looked across to see that my husband was peacefully asleep. Deciding against waking him up, I pondered on the dream for a moment, smiled and went back to sleep again, still smiling.

Allow me to share a few lessons that I have learnt from Papa and Mama over the years that I have known them. These are lessons learnt both from what they taught me and also from them just living their life without having to say much.

The quote by St. Francis of Assisi, which says, **"Preach the gospel at all times and when necessary, use words"** sums up their lives for me.

Papa Myles Munroe

GENUINE LOVE FOR PEOPLE

Papa not only talked about love for people...ALL people, but he showed it and lived it. I have realised that it is more difficult to try to be something that you are not than to just be yourself. The truth is much easier to maintain because you do not have to actually think about new things to do or say all the time; unlike when you are not being truthful - consistency can be a challenge. Mom and Dad loved all people from different races, cultures, creeds, backgrounds, dispositions, religions, rich, poor, educated, illiterate, young, old, etc. His quote, "Always reduce everyone to a human being", was exactly how they lived. They even loved my husband and I and our kids unconditionally. In all the time we had the privilege to be with them, this was our experience.

Papa, at your home-going service, Charlie Masala spoke and said something that resonated with me and testified to my experience. He said that "…your love for people was so genuine and focused for each individual that whenever you were with an individual, that individual felt like he/she was the most important person in your life"; and the whole place just broke out in the agreement. You had the ability to make us all feel like that. This was not just Charlie's experience but every other human being, all over the world, who had the privilege of having you in their life. **You loved deliberately and relentlessly!** You were not quick to 'write-off' a person because they showed weakness; rather you were always willing to offer the option of rehabilitation and reconciliation before anything else.

It was that love that drew me to you, even before I heard your message. From the first time I met you, I felt love and acceptance. After the Sunday service on the eve of the Leadership Summit in 2009, you spent some time with us, chatting, laughing and taking photos with us like you had known us for years. I was stunned at first and at that moment, I knew you were different. I knew that not a lot of 'leaders' are people-persons. They normally prefer to speak and then have their waiting bodyguards escort them from the podium, before or without having to socialise with the people. You were different. You had no bodyguards and were open to and welcomed everybody - even me! You always said your only bodyguard was your wife and that you did not need another. Anybody could approach you. I did not have to try to be smart, to try and say the 'right' things or even rehearse my words when approaching you. I did not have to try and be something I am not with you, I felt safe enough to just be myself. You made me feel that being myself was both okay and enough. You did not know us and had never heard of us before and yet you loved! You didn't even have to say the words. You were able to love everyone the same because to you everybody was a human being. You were very observant and you hardly forgot a face and the story behind the face. That is one of the greatest challenges you have left me with. I strive to be to other people what you were and still are to me, my family and millions more. Your life has shown me this is possible.

HUMBLE AND HUMOROUS

For a man of your stature, you surely were larger than life. When you walked into a room, people definitely noticed. You just could not be ignored. You unintentionally commanded recognition. You worked hard and played just as hard. One of our most memorable times was when sharing a meal, whether in a restaurant or at your home. You had your own funny way of saying grace: "Father forgive us for what we are about to do….!" Like you expected that we might overdo it, so better ask for forgiveness before, right? You genuinely appreciated food to the extent of saying, "This food is so good it must come straight from the Kingdom…" You went on to chat with and even pray for the people that waited on us, making them feel special and necessary. You would get their name and address them saying "Thank you so much for serving us"; "If you were not here this place and indeed our experience would not be the same, God bless you". Those people would walk away surprised but having a permanent grin on their faces. In October 2014 while in Durban and getting ready to leave for Johannesburg, we were walking through the airport towards the jet and somehow, I must have slowed down a bit because you caught me staring at a beautiful outfit on display at one of the shops. You almost jumped at me as you grabbed my hand and pulled me forward and away from that shop saying, "Be strong now, look ahead. Do not allow yourself to be distracted..." By this time I was laughing uncontrollably because earlier on you saw me coming for lunch holding a Woolworths shopping bag and laughed as you pointed at me saying, "You look guilty". Then to my husband, "Eric, look at her. She looks guilty... guilty of shopping". I had only bought one pair of shoes (*sigh*). This time around I couldn't understand how you saw that, but then again, you were always very observant Papa. Nothing escaped you. As we continued walking you said jokingly, "your husband must thank me now, I've just saved him money" and we laughed as went to join the others.

'NEVER SAY DIE' ATTITUDE

Sometimes I would ask myself if you ever got tired. I mean, I know you obviously would because you were human but you hardly showed it. You were like a 'permanently fully-charged battery' that just would not die. I remember on the 12th of October, 2014, we had just landed in Johannesburg from Durban where you had preached a total of about 3 different sermons and Mama had preached that same morning at a different church. In just over 24 hours, you had ministered to thousands of people and upon landing, we were rushed to another meeting in Sandton where you were scheduled to speak to masses. After that meeting, we rushed to attend a 20th Wedding Anniversary celebration where you were the keynote speaker. By this time we were all seriously exhausted but when you spoke, you gave it your all. It was as if that was your first speaking engagement of the day. You did not break a sweat, you did not complain and your countenance remained intact, just as it had been that morning. You and Mama remained as graceful as ever throughout the approximately 3 to 4-hour event. You even stayed a little while longer after the festivities were over and socialised with the guests. We finally left for the hotel around midnight.

We got to the hotel after midnight and Eric and I still had to get our car and drive for another 90 minutes to get home. Upon arrival, Mama said her goodnight and quickly disappeared into the elevator, which was totally understandable. She was exhausted. You stuck around with us while we waited for our car and joked around about still feeling quite fit to go another mile. I looked on in utter disbelief as you proceeded to playfully challenge us while mimicking boxing moves saying, "I still have energy man. I'm ready to go. Who wants to go another mile with me?" As we looked on, we were getting more and more exhausted, wondering where you alone get the unfair advantage of the 'extra dose of energy' that the rest of us don't have access to. As you continued to bounce around, somewhat like Mohammed Ali, suddenly it hit me and I had to admit to myself that in all my many years on this earth, I had never met anybody like you.

Just as I was about to write you off as an 'extra-terrestrial' being, as we walked into the hotel lobby, you stopped and almost whispering you said to us, "Jokes aside ya'll, I am exhausted! I am so looking forward to sleeping and boy, am I gonna sleep. I going to sleep and snore so loud ya'll gonna hear me snoring from your home." There was that sense of humour again and at the weirdest moment; we laughed...loud! I think the hotel staff at the lobby must have thought we had taken leave of our senses. I looked at you then and I could actually see fatigue in your eyes even though you were laughing and wondered how you pulled it off. How did you manage to hide it for so long? Anyway, we said our goodbyes and began the drive home; laughing all the way at the thought of hearing you snore while we slept 150 kilometres away.

I was really challenged that day. This is just one example out of many. All the time we spent with you whenever you came to South Africa was quite special. We would eagerly anticipate the late nights and late dinners after sessions where we would stuff our faces while you continued to impart invaluable wisdom in our lives. Those are memories I will forever treasure and hold close to my heart. You spoke into our marriages, to us as individuals, about the state of the world, the challenges facing our governments and solutions to those challenges and gladly answered all our questions. Of course, after the late nights came early mornings! Back to work again and you were just as energetic in the morning as you were the night before. In hindsight, I must admit that spending that time with you always felt like an 'affectionate boot camp'. We learnt a lot from you (the words you spoke) and through you (the way you conducted yourself). You were always unperturbed and very agile. You had the ability to adapt to any situation seamlessly without compromising your values and integrity. I admired that in you and would often quietly say to myself, "When I grow up I want to be like that."

You have left such an indelible mark not just in me but in all the individuals that have known you personally. Even though you are no longer physically here with us, you continue to teach, educate, lead and mentor us through your books, audios, DVDs and other material. Your legacy lives on and will forever do so. You would often say, **"The greatest act of leadership is what happens in your absence.** If all you have done dies with you, you are a failure. True leadership is measured by what happens after you die."

I would say then Papa, that you Sir are a true leader!!

MAN OF CHARACTER

"My life is my message". - Mahatma Gandhi

You would often say you always travel with your wife and children because they were your message. You said with them around you, you were preaching without having to say a word! Wow!

Papa, you didn't just teach me but you also showed me how my husband ought to love me just by loving Mama the way you did. You made Mama feel so secure in your love for her and that gave her confidence beyond measure (she told me), to be whatever she needed to be to enable you to fulfil your purpose. She found the freedom 'to be' or 'to become' in the safety and security of your unconditional love for her. You publicly declared your love for Mama and your children every chance you got and told them how proud you are of them. You often said, "My wife is my bodyguard. That is why I always travel with her".

In 2013 at the Global Leadership Summit, you taught on the importance of character in a leaders' life. You said, "Character is the quality which is unchanging, stable and dependable. The more your secret place becomes public, the closer you are to character", "Live your life in such a way that your silence is heavier than your words" and "Don't prepare a sermon, prepare your life". You really lived what you preached. You never changed, whether it was an abruptly cancelled appointment, a delayed or cancelled flight, flying coach, speaking at back-to-back sessions or just sheer fatigue, you remained! You led by example and with love, inspiring us to relentlessly pursue our purpose and find the Creator's original intent for our lives. You also cautioned us that it is possible to discover one's purpose but still not be convicted enough to pursue it. That was a wake-up call for me.

Before I met you I believed in the death penalty. I've always thought, for example, that if a person intentionally and maliciously takes another person's life, then that person does not deserve to keep theirs. But you taught me that love goes a long way and is superior to revenge. You also taught me that the pursuit of righteousness is superior to the pursuit of wealth. At your home-going service, Charlie Masala spoke words that attested to your character. He said, "It's been 3 weeks since he's been gone and there has been no scandal".

PURPOSE-DRIVEN

You and Mama both **personified** your definition of 'leadership' in my life…"Leadership is the capacity to influence others through inspiration, motivated by passion, generated by vision, produced by a conviction, ignited by a purpose".

I remember a day in October 2013 when we were flying back from

Uganda to South Africa and we were experiencing above normal turbulence. Most of us had started to doze off since we were quite exhausted from the sessions. I think I must have looked worried because when you opened your eyes and looked at me, you smiled reassuringly and said, "Don't worry my daughter; my purpose is too great for this plane to crash today and the fact that you are here with me means that you too are safe". Almost immediately after saying that, you dozed off again. I was left with two choices; to worry and not enjoy the ride or to believe what you had just said for my own life. I chose the latter and was amazed at the peace that came with that decision. Little did I know then that your words would help someone else even after you had gone. Three days after your home-going service, Eric and I left the Bahamas and flew back to South Africa. On that particular flight, we could not get seats that allowed us to sit together, so he sat one row behind me. I sat between two ladies and we introduced ourselves and started to chat. A few hours into the flight, we started to feel the most horrifying turbulence I had ever experienced. It went on and off for long periods at a time. It was so bad that it felt to me as though the aircraft would break in half. I remained unperturbed and at peace and as I looked to my left, the lady sitting next to me looked as white as a sheet. She looked like she had seen a ghost and stopped breathing a few moments ago. She had the most petrified look on her face. I remembered our conversation and carefully moved my left hand and put it over hers to reassure her, without saying a word at first. Then when I realised that that was not working as much as I thought it would, I put my left arm around her shoulders and my right hand over her left hand, pulled her closer to me and firmly said these words to her, "My purpose is too great for this plane to crash and the fact that you are here with me means that you too are safe, because this aircraft is not going down with me in it…not today". For a few seconds, she had the most bewildered expression on her face. I couldn't decide whether it was because she was thinking, "How can this stranger be so presumptuous?" or she just decided to believe what I had just said for her own life. So I decided it was the latter. Now facing her directly, I repeated the sentence two or three more times until I saw her shoulders and contorted face literally start to relax. She smiled at me and said a heartfelt, "Thank you." It was only then that I felt immense pressure on my hand and realised that she had been holding on to it very tightly.

You pursued your purpose with uncompromising conviction. Even at the time of your transition from the earth, you were on your way to doing just that. One speaker at your home-going attested to this. He said he had once asked you how you are able to do what you do and do it the way you do it. How are you able to consistently and tirelessly give of yourself such that you continue to become relevant to the world? To this question, you answered, "Do birds fly?" He said he was a little confused at first until he realised that you meant you were only doing what you were built to do and therefore, like a bird or a fish, neither of them can get tired flying or swimming because that would mean they are tired of being themselves. The speaker went on to share another question that he had the privilege of asking you. He asked what you would do if your wife were to pass on before you. And to this, your answer was, "Mourn I would but preach I must". Wow, that just really spoke to me personally. Even after you were gone you were still teaching me that purpose is more important than the events that happen or don't happen during the course of our life. The events are transitory but the purpose is not, so no event should be given the power to interfere with our assignment.

There are no appropriate words we can use to describe the pain that the reality of your absence presents but we also take courage in the invaluable legacy you left us with. You will always live on in our hearts.

> "I don't want my name on a building that a hurricane will tear down but in the leadership of those I mentor"
>
> - MYLES E. MUNROE

Mama Ruth Ann Munroe

Quiet, confident, gentle and full of wisdom. How greatly privileged I am to have known you!

YOU KNEW WHO YOU WERE

You told us that people would often ask you what your assignment or purpose was, seeing that you were already married to the 'man of purpose' himself. You shared how you would simply reply, "My assignment is my husband", meaning that you were born to be anything, everything, at anytime and anywhere that your husband needed for him to fulfil his purpose. I thought that was amazing. I remember thinking to myself, "Wow, I've never thought of my role as a wife that way before and it makes so much sense". I realised then that all you were saying was that you were his helper - and that was your purpose. Yet you were also confident that in no way did this take away from you. I also do realise that this is something that society generally frowns upon. I will forever treasure our conversations and your advice on various topics, mostly on marriage, parenting and healthy living, certainly not forgetting our numerous 'shopping sprees'. I already miss those a lot! I miss how you, Charisa, Zoli and I would sneak off during breaks, especially during lunchtime and go shopping for garbs and accessories for the evening event or just for no particular reason except shopping of course! Once we told Papa we were going to the mall, he would jokingly mutter under his breath, "Oh Lord, have mercy on me please", in anticipation of 'the damage' to his bank account when we come back.

STRONG AND CONFIDENT

Even though Papa was the one sought after by the crowds, leaving you standing all alone at times, you remained unperturbed. Often crowds of people would 'steal' Papa away from you; be it for a quick photo, a last-minute question or conversation, an autograph, an introduction to a friend or family member…the list is unending. Through all this, I watched in awe as you kept your composure, unthreatened, secure and very content; your smile never waning. I had observed that about you from the first time I met you in 2009 when I came to the Bahamas to attend the Leadership Summit for the first time. As I continued to observe you over the years, it quickly became apparent to me that I also wanted that virtue. I had to admit to myself that I was not sure I would handle myself the same way if I was in the same situation.

From where I stood, you were always well-poised, calm, confident and composed. I now know, as you told me in one of our last conversations, that, that was the case because you knew that Papa loved you and you felt secure in his love. You added that this security did not come only because he told you he loved you every so often, but that there were other things he constantly did and said, both privately and publicly that further anchored that love. So, just like a queen who knows her rightful position in the palace, you were unruffled by 'visitors' and naysayers, because you knew your position when it came to your husband.

BEAUTY AND GRACE

You always looked gorgeous! How on earth did you manage that? You radiated beauty from the inside out. From formal events all the way to Safari trips in the various game parks, you always 'pulled it off'. Always! You represented and complimented your husband exquisitely, yet keeping your calm, tranquil and collected self. I could say that you constantly had 'your wits about you'. Even though I was still learning a lot from you when our fellowship was abruptly cut short, I hope and pray that the lessons I learnt will also enrich my marriage. Papa was a very happy, jovial, confident, 'ready-to-go' guy who was full of energy and a rich sense of humour; and I believe that was almost entirely your fault ☺. The way you lived your life and especially the way you related to Papa, made me believe what I once thought was almost impossible could be within reach – the Proverbs 31 woman. I know that he could go on and on the way he did because you, his biggest fan, were always there to cheer him on. Without you by his side, I personally do not think he would have been able to do as much of what he did with seamless vigour, determination and purpose.

GENEROUS AND SELFLESS

You shared your husband and family with the rest of the world. You could only do this because you too understood and aligned yourself with purpose. You would often go to bed and leave us still chatting with Papa, sometimes until the wee hours of the morning. I'm not sure I know a lot of women who would do that. The Leadership Summit would not be complete without you gathering all of us from different countries at your home to cook the Sunday meal for us and you never broke a sweat. The food was good…really good. We were treated to various palatable Bahamian cuisines, especially the guava duff ☺, which we especially enjoyed. The food was so good that we just refused to leave while it was still there, not even after Papa's attempts to get us back to our hotel, citing that it's late and we needed to be up early for the morning session. There was so much love and acceptance, a true sense of belonging. I really, really miss those times!

I understand that all the time spent with you presented us with opportunities to learn and that is the best part. You both made such an indelible deposit in us; your legacy is undeniable. Indeed, "Life is not measured by duration but by donation".

www.ingramcontent.com/pod-product-compliance
Lightning Source LLC
LaVergne TN
LVHW051638080426
835511LV00016B/2375